LIZ LEWINSON

WOMEN
MEDITATION
AND
POWER

Other books by Liz Lewinson

American Buddhist Rebel:
The Story of Rama - Dr. Frederick Lenz

Independence Ring

LIZ LEWINSON

WOMEN
MEDITATION
AND
POWER

SKYE
PEARL

Copyright © 2020 by Liz Lewinson
Women, Meditation, and Power

Published 2020 by Skye Pearl
Sausalito, CA USA

ISBN: 978-0-9898899-2-6 (Paperback)
ISBN: 978-0-9898899-4-0 (eBook)

> Publisher's Cataloging-In-Publication Data
> (Prepared by The Donohue Group, Inc.)
>
> Names: Lewinson, Liz, author.
> Title: Women, meditation, and power / Liz Lewinson.
> Description: [Second edition]. | Sausalito, CA, USA : Skye Pearl, 2020. | Includes bibliographical references.
> Identifiers: ISBN 9780989889926 (paperback) | ISBN 9780989889940 (ebook)
> Subjects: LCSH: Feminism--United States. | Femininity. | Feminist theory. | Social role. | Power (Social sciences) | Sex role. | Meditation. | BISAC: SOCIAL SCIENCE / Women's Studies. | SOCIAL SCIENCE / Gender Studies. | SOCIAL SCIENCE / Feminism & Feminist Theory.
> Classification: LCC HQ1421 .L42 2020 (print) | LCC HQ1421 (ebook) | DDC 305.42/0973--dc23

ALL RIGHTS RESERVED

The scanning, uploading and distribution of this book via the Internet or via any other means without the permission of the publisher is illegal and punishable by law. Please purchase only authorized electronic editions, and do not participate in or encourage electronic piracy of copyrighted materials. Your support of the author's rights is appreciated.

The Author and the Publisher accept no responsibility for inaccuracies or omissions, and speci ically disclaim any liability, loss, or risk, whether personal, inancial, or otherwise, that is incurred as a consequence, directly or indirectly, from the use and/or application of any of the contents of this book.

Cover art by Brains & Riots Creative Studio

This book is dedicated to the power of women and to my Buddhist teacher, who first divulged the elephant in the room.

CONTENTS

Introduction xi

1: The First Satori (Realization) 1

2: Positively Powerful 13

3: Power Paradigms for Women 21

4: Meditation Class #1 — Power 27

5: The Tsunami and the Diamond Mind 33

6: Meditation Class #2 — Heart 41

7: Love and Humility for Men 45

8: People: Serena Williams 47

9: Gender Mix-Up! 53

10: People: Malala Yousafzai 63

11: Meditation Class #3 — Intellect 69

12: Gender Mistakes 71

13: People: Zhou Qunfei 89

14: The Sex Koan 93

15: Meditation Class #4 — Hints and Tips . . 103

16: Married/Partnered, Single Ladies 107

17: A Fine Tool Chest 115

18: Meditation Class #5 — Environment . . . 135

19: People: Michelle Obama 139

20: Breakups, Breakthroughs and Mindfulness . . 145

21: Visualization Technique 151

22: Viking Leaders 153

23: Knowledge 157

Liz Lewinson 163

I'm a woman
Phenomenally.
Phenomenal woman,
That's me.

— Maya Angelou

INTRODUCTION

> What is the difference between men and women? Women are more powerful.
>
> **—Dr. Frederick Lenz**

This book is for all genders and is focused on women, in whatever form that takes. How much "woman" you have in your being is yours to decide. We all have both female and male inside us, and ultimately, as you evolve in your meditation practice, there is no gender difference. For most of us, however, there is a leading gender imprint. In this book, I primarily write about the female person.

O female person, this is what you need to understand. Yes, you are strong. More opportunities are opening. Male hypocrisy is being exposed and busted. But is your internal operating system keeping up to date? With each new revelation, are you clearly shedding another deep-rooted layer of powerlessness? If not, this book will help you look deeper.

Women are the power species on planet Earth. We are the leaders, the strategists, the negotiators, the collaborators, the seers, the matriarchs. We are naturally excellent at experiencing inner stillness—the ultimate nexus and balancing center of life power.

Women today are rising from thousands of years of repression. Women are shattering glass ceilings and previous perceptions of what women can and should accomplish. The women shattering glass ceilings are those who find a way to express their power and energy, fighting to achieve this all the way. They bring a peerless power and energy to their tasks.

The adolescent girls of today are the leaders of tomorrow. But if their education is neglected, if they are given inappropriate knowledge about their own abilities and potential, then the results are disastrous for the planet. Girls in so-called liberated nations often face a crisis in their teen years. It's when being sexually and physically attractive to boys or other girls often trumps becoming educated and powerful.

Westernized teens, with all that built-in energy and power that come with a strong, young nervous system, often weaken it with destructive and unfulfilling sex, bullying, violence, drugs, and overfocus on what others are doing instead of building confidence in self. The result is a long confusion period, especially for women, in which it takes years to regain the state of energy and assuredness that was lost in the teen years. Some women never regain it and instead make poor choices that burden them for the rest of their lives.

Regaining or understanding for the first time their full, unlimited power is, for most women, a journey of identifying and overcoming past restraints.

This book begins with my story of how I untwisted the vines of mental fantasy that were keeping me from perceiving my potential or even a desire to achieve my potential. To be honest, I first heard about gender truth when I attended several talks by a Buddhist teacher. It was he who told it like it is. But to my credit, I "got it."

Time has passed since I heard him speak on the vast, innate power of women, and I am still "getting it." I look constantly with fresh eyes at the men and women around me and the assumptions that falsely hold us in place.

I have practiced meditation for many years. Meditation is about making the mind still and quiet, and after you have been meditating for a while, your intuition greatly increases. You can "see" what is going on around you in ways that were not possible before. With just a glance, you imbibe information about people you interact with, and even if it's only a brief interaction, you can "see" and sense into their souls.

I was at the filming of a Deepak Chopra workshop not long ago. He has his own lovely film space on the second floor of ABC Carpet and Home in Manhattan. The store offers a high-end collection of esoteric household items that have something in common—they are all refined and beautiful. Deepak's studio continues the theme of tasteful elegance with yoga-themed artwork and contemporary, brightly colored furnishings on the stage.

When I arrived about ten minutes early, the hall was packed, primarily with women ranging in age from their twenties to their fifties, with the younger age span predominating. I took my seat and began to look around. I'm always interested in how women feel and dress and express their high-power energy.

This was a yoga crowd, a distinctive demographic. Good posture, tasteful but not loud garb, neat but not flashy hairstyles. The room was filled with intelligent people aspiring to know more and be more. All were sufficiently affluent to pay the twenty-five- dollar cover charge.

The lady sitting in front of me had a beautiful, straight yoga back, probably the result of countless hours in an exercise studio. She stood up to use the ladies' room, and I studied her face as she returned. I took my instant intuitive snapshot of her mental and emotional state. Damn. She was deferent, insecure, and drained. Something or someone in her life was kicking the spark out of her. As many uplifting Deepak talks she might attend, unless she removed the internal boulder that blocked her attaining and recognizing her own unbounded power, she would stay stuck in the shoals of self-doubt and low energy. I looked at her and thought, 'We, as women, are truly not there yet.'

I did not look at every woman in the audience but sensed that many had deep self-confidence issues, which manifested in their overall weak vibrations. I knew these were good people and they were all seeking more awareness, which made them in my eyes very good people. Yet, instead of sitting in a lotus, I was sitting in an issue.

That issue is—

**WE WOMEN
DO NOT
GET
HOW POWERFUL
WE
INNATELY ARE.**

We just don't get it yet. And as long as we don't get it, we won't seek to manifest ultimate power—that we women are so good at and that the planet needs desperately—to achieve health.

If we do not recognize our own vast female power, we won't appreciate and recognize it in other women.

In 2016, the United States held an election. A capable, highly educated, experienced, and wise politician, Hillary Clinton, was pitted against a misogynistic dictator-in-waiting, Donald Trump. Donald won, not the popular vote but the electoral vote. It was reported that many women did not vote for Hillary. These women said they did not "trust" her. Instead, they voted for an emotional toddler, a buffoon, a lout, an intellectual pygmy. His only saving grace was being male.

People did not trust Hillary because she is a woman. This is horrific sexism. Women know about it and still fall into the trap of expressing it. And it really has to stop.

Women running for the office of president of the United States are asked about their "likeability factor." Men do not get asked that.

The notion that men are better at governing or in any role involving the use of power and deep judgment is a farce. It is false.

Women are inherently suited to express, manifest, and lead with power. No caveats are required.

1

THE FIRST SATORI (REALIZATION)

> We need to reshape our own perception of how we view ourselves. We have to step up as women and take the lead.
>
> —**Beyoncé**

Los Angeles is a petri dish of nascent ideas.

I lived in Los Angeles, a city where everyone sampled spiritual teachers. Lampposts in the college town of Westwood, near the University of California at Los Angeles (UCLA), were festooned with posters of Eastern and Western teachers offering forms of traditional or New Age wisdom. On a night when I had nothing to do—that was most nights—I agreed to meet my friend Eva to hear an American Buddhist teacher.

At the time, I eked out a living as a freelance journalist, but I figured I did not have to earn a high income because someday I would meet Mr. Right and *he* would have a high income. I yearned for marriage and kids, and even though I had been in romantic relationships, one lasting four years, none had resulted in a "Will you marry me?" My obvious inadequacy was a source of daily self-bullying.

That night, I forced myself to get dressed and go out. I slung on some jeans, a long-sleeved blouse, and enough makeup to look attractive just in case. Eva, an old friend who always seemed cheerful and upbeat, told me the talk would help my depression. But I knew it would be another night of embarrassment, filled with committed and steady couples, while I would be stuck by myself, trying to look content, or hanging out with Eva, making it clear I couldn't get a man.

Turning the key in my Mazda's ignition, I sighed. When would I meet the man who would sweep me off my feet and take care of me, one who would find in me the fascinating and alluring creature I knew myself to be (given the right romantic circumstances)?

Variations of this tape played over and over in my head.

It took about twenty minutes to drive from my apartment in Santa Monica to Beverly Hills. At the theatre, I saw a line of women stretched around the block. I saw very few men. I found my friend Eva in line.

"I'm so glad you could come," she trilled. She was in her element, spiritual teacher-land.

That night when the teacher walked onto the theatre's art deco stage, I did a visual double take. My idea of a "teacher" was firmly etched in old, Asian, and robed. Instead, this guy was dressed simply in college professor garb. He was young, tall, nice looking—OK, seriously cute. He sat on a small couch in the middle of the stage and shuffled quietly through files on a narrow table next to the couch. As he did that, I felt him taking the temperature of the audience.

I settled into the plush movie-theatre seat—who knew what this person would say?

He greeted everyone evenly, then posited questions: "Why don't more women attain enlightenment? Why is it that most of the enlightened teachers that people have heard of are men? Why are women lagging behind men in positions of authority and power?"

"OK," I thought, "that was a good opening. Let's see what he has in his deck of cards."

He then explained that the reason more women don't attain enlightenment, are held back, and do not comprehend how powerful they are is cultural. It has to do with recent history (the last few thousand years) and mental conditioning.

"OK," I thought. "This is definitely interesting." I rummaged through my handbag, searching for a pen and notepaper.

This is what he said.

From a spiritual point of view, women exemplify power.

Men have reacted very negatively to the power that is inherent in women. Rather than realizing that they have the same power, only it manifests in other ways, they have rejected it and sought to convince women of the exact opposite, that they are powerless.

I looked up at the stage. He was talking in a quiet, natural tone, as if "doesn't everyone know this?" This was the early 1980s. No, most people did not know about this.

He said men have convinced women of their powerlessness through sexual repression, economic repression, political repression, social repression, ideological repression, and spiritual repression.

Wow, *repression*. Strong word. It was not a word I used a lot. He didn't lighten up on it either.

He said women have been taught that they are not powerful. As a matter of fact, they've been given an opposite description—that they are weak. In a world of darkness, men have taught them this because they were afraid, because the thing men want the most, they fear the most—power.

When you wish to subjugate a people, you have to convince them of their own inherent weakness. If they believe they are weak, they will not rebel. If they believe they are strong and intelligent, they will rebel.

Suddenly, this was a lot to digest. I wasn't a revolutionary. I paid my taxes. I walked across streets on the crosswalks fairly often.

I instead focused on one sentence. "Women exemplify power." What did that mean? In my professional career to date, I had met one woman I thought of as powerful. She ran her own public relations company and had earned the respect of her industry. The rest—no. They were perfectly content to let men take the lead. They went just so far, then stopped, politely allowing their male partners or colleagues to stay ahead of them in some respect.

I learned more truth that night.

Men and women have energy bodies that surround their physical bodies. And they are different, just as men's and women's physical bodies are different. The teacher called the energy body that surrounds the physical body the "subtle physical body."

I was fine with that concept. I was aware that people radiate energies that extend beyond their physical body. I could feel them. For example, if someone was angry, I could sense and feel it just standing near them, and their emotions affected me as well. If someone was cheerful, I could sense and feel that.

He explained that while both a man's and woman's energy bodies are composed of luminous fibers of light, the subtle physical body of a woman conducts light or vibrates with light at a different rate than that of a man's.

The subtle physical bodies of men are denser. They're much more tightly packed. The subtle physical body of a woman is much more pliant. Pure life force flows through a woman's energy body much more rapidly and readily.

As a visual, he said that the energy surround–ing the male body is held closer to the physical body and is more compact and grid-like. The energy of a woman looks like a butterfly's wings extending way out from her body, moving rapidly. It is fluid in appearance and composition.

Because of this difference, a man is well suited to express the qualities of love and humility, while a woman is innately suited to express power.

I took a deep breath.

I could picture that. I suddenly thought about powerful events in nature that are characterized by rapid movement and change. The faster the change, the more powerful the event. If women were innately wired for more rapid movement and change—processing life force more rapidly than men—then they indeed represented power.

"It's all mixed up," I thought.

As soon as I had that thought, the teacher said, "Everything is reversed in this age. Men appear to be more powerful than women, while the opposite is really true."

He pointed out that there is a natural tendency in human nature to attempt to destroy what one is threatened by. Thus men, threatened by the power of women, have tried to destroy it in every way. They'd been successful at doing this for millennia such that women today have deep mental conditioning and habits about their apparent powerlessness.

The imbalance that exists today between men and women is the primary cause of the violence and disorder we now see in the world.

His words spun in my head. I had not thought of myself as repressed before, but I also had not thought of myself as very powerful. I had accepted as fact that men were more powerful. It had never occurred to me that the gender with the natural, inherent ability to express and deal with power was female.

Suddenly, seated in the hall, I found myself pulling out a mental checklist of my subliminal gender assumptions.

Just two hours earlier, I had been desperate to find a male partner who was more powerful—stronger, more influential, and wealthier than me—and now I'd just learned that power was on my side of the chessboard. I would *not* find a man (in spite of his outer achievements) more powerful than me because he did not exist. I was the power gender.

There was one more zinger that night.

The teacher pointed out there are many ways to give selflessly, and having children is only one of them. For some women seeking to try different things in this lifetime, it may not be the right choice. If you have children, he said, you should do a wonderful job of raising them. It is an excellent path, but he advised not to lose yourself in your children. Keep your own powerful identity.

If you did not have children, he suggested you consider forgoing it. There were already billons of people on the planet. Women could help the planet by developing their own power levels and focusing on leadership in all the arenas where they had previously been repressed.

When I left the talk that night, an amazing thing happened. Somehow, my inner marriage tape stopped. Once my mind stopped chattering, I gained a new perspective. Suddenly, marriage was a choice, a "maybe."

When the premise of giving selflessly in other ways than having children was presented, my obsession with the biological clock disappeared.

I pulled back into my Santa Monica driveway that night, shorn of ideas that had imprinted me since I'd watched *Cinderella* in second grade. Think about it—her stepmother and stepsisters hate her because she is beautiful. A prince falls in love with her because she is beautiful. Part of her charm is her tiny feet that can fit into little glass slippers which turn out to be the key to capturing the prince, getting married, and living happily ever after. The prince will take care of her for the rest of her life. No. Wrong.

Suddenly, I felt inspired to explore power levels I had not considered before and to do it on my own.

I felt vibrant and energized by suddenly becoming unchained. The false enchantment had lifted. My comatose self dozing off in powerlessness had just been kissed on the lips, not by a prince but by a simple truth.

I thought I would still "date," but the all-encompassing pressure bubble—to be swept off my feet, to get the bridal dress, the party, the ring, the soul mate (or at least someone reasonable)—was punctured.

And yes, the planet was in deep ecological trouble, but perhaps I could offer a personal solution related to restoring gender balance and helping ease violence and disorder in the world.

In the place of constant self-nagging and doubt: sudden stillness.

2

POSITIVELY POWERFUL

> This journey has always been about reach-
> ing your own other shore no matter what it
> is, and that dream continues.
>
> —**Diana Nyad**

Domination, rigidity, suppression, smashing, crashing, destroying, repression, overthrowing, limiting (the dictionary definitions of power)—no wonder the word "power" has a bad rep! Abuse of power in the last couple of thousand years has been symptomatic of people (99.99 percent men) who have achieved some level of worldly status.

Over time, however, as my power level has grown, I've became comfortable with the term "power" as I witness and experience it. To understand more about power, I turned to the writings of others.

> The most common way people give up their power is by thinking they don't have any.
>
> —Alice Walker

> As you enter positions of trust and power, dream a little before you think.
>
> —Toni Morrison

> To call woman the weaker sex is a libel; it is man's injustice to woman.
>
> If by strength is meant brute strength, then, indeed, is woman less brute than man. If by strength is meant moral power, then woman is immeasurably man's superior.
>
> Has she not greater intuition, is she not more self-sacrificing, has she not greater powers of endurance, has she not greater courage?
>
> Without her, man could not be.

> If nonviolence is the law of our being, the future is with woman. Who can make a more effective appeal to the heart than woman?
>
> —Mahatma Gandhi

> There is no limit to what we, as women, can accomplish, whether that's in politics or other fields.
>
> —Michelle Obama

And I perused the dictionary for good explanations. "Power" in its simplest definition from the *Merriam-Webster Dictionary* is "the ability to act or produce an effect." That's all. This is the kind of power we are discussing here—the ability to act with clarity, wisdom, and compassion to produce a positive, beneficial effect.

The *Encarta* dictionary states, "Power is the capacity to do something," but look at the synonyms:

- Physical force

    —Not a female definition of power.

- Control and influence over other people

    —Control linked with influence implies a corrupted definition.

- Authority to act
    —Seems reasonable.
- Persuasiveness
    —Also reasonable.

The Microsoft Word for Windows program lists these synonyms for power: authority, control, influence, supremacy, rule, command, clout, and muscle. I looked at these critically.

- Authority
    —What does that mean?
    Where are the limits?
- Control
    —Over whom and what? When?
    Easy to abuse.
- Influence
    —Definitely an attribute of power.
- Supremacy
    —Does not sound like a female view of working with power.
- Rule
    —How? What kind of rule?
- Commanding

- —Maybe, depending on how it would be done and how frequently.
- Muscle
  - —Fit and strong is fine, but "muscle" as used to "muscle" people out of something or dominate people of lesser physical strength—not good, but slow and low.

Nowhere does "fluidity" appear, even though rapid transformation is the essence of natural power.

This is what I mean by examining the subtle imprints of gender bias we have all been stamped with. The definitions of power in the world today are loaded toward men.

> Power is extreme, wise, compassionate fluidity.
>
> —Liz Lewinson

I began to observe the energy bodies of men and women. What is an energy body? Everything and everyone has one. A rock has one. A chicken has one. Men and women have them. It is the energy or vibration that projects beyond physical mass.

"I always feel good around Mary."

> She projects out beyond her physical body the energy of happiness, positivity, buoyancy.

"I always feel anxious around Tim."

> He projects out beyond his physical body the feelings of stress, worry, and anxiety.

Sensing energy surrounding a physical object or being is done by "feeling," not thinking.

Couples, groups of men, groups of women, people working out in the gym, people at shopping malls and beaches. A person walking by in the park, hands in pockets, engrossed in thought. You can tell a lot about people by "feeling" quietly.

I watched quietly and saw who was more animated, flowing, more mutable. It was the woman every time. To me, this meant women were more powerful. But did the women I observed understand what this meant? Did they own power? I rarely saw that.

Power can be wielded for great good, and that's the kind of power we're talking about. Bill and Melinda Gates use their success and financial influence to assist the world. Oprah uses celebrity power for good. Michelle Obama uses political power to benefit others. Mother Meera, a spiritual teacher based in Germany, uses spiritual power to help others. They all become *more* powerful by sharing power.

When you are told you are innately and incredibly powerful as a woman, what does that mean? Women need to forge a new definition of power based on themselves and become that new definition.

Women represent power in the natural world of inner cosmography. If women are not perceived and recognized in that way, and if women themselves do not perceive that, then there is an ongoing blockage of energy for men, women, and the planet.

3

THE TSUNAMI AND THE DIAMOND MIND

> A river of Truth
> Ends at a dam of bias—
> Truth floods and moves on.
>
> **—Gloria Steinem**

Not long ago, for my job as a technology project manager, I travelled to Germany to meet with local users of a new banking system. While I was there, I planned a side trip to a small town outside of Frankfurt to visit a woman teacher. She meets with her students and visitors in an old castle that has been turned into a meditation hall. I had a very powerful meditation experience with Mother Meera; my mind was still and clear for weeks afterward.

I flew back to New York City in the late afternoon, took a cab from JFK Airport to the city, and opened the door to my one-bedroom apartment in midtown Manhattan. As I stood in the nondescript small foyer, I felt I had stepped into a geographical void.

A question arose in my mind. "What is the visual symbol for what I have been observing all these years—that men are actually built for love and humility and women are built for power?"

All of a sudden, I found myself transposed to a very different place.

I stood on a thin sliver of beach. Directly in front of me shimmered a vast wall of water, a huge tsunami wave, fully risen. The wave was so tall that I could barely see the crest, as if I were gazing toward the top of a skyscraper. At its distant height, foam flew off its crest. I heard a deep, megawatt roar emanating from the wave's liquid gray-green depths. All sounds were melded into it—whistling, singing, drumming, laughing, yelling, shrieking—one huge roar. I felt its incredible, pulsing, liquid power.

I "knew" that this tsunami, risen to its highest peak, was capable of taking any form. It stretched on forever. I knew there was no end to it. I felt it. I felt it all through my body, this incredible, fluid, pulsing, roaring power. There is no other word to describe it. It was pure, raw power. I knew THIS was the symbol of women's power—intense beyond measure, roaring, fluid, vast, and boundless.

Since this was not my imagination at work—I really was standing before an incredible vertical, throbbing skyscraper of deep, glimmering water poised to crash down—I barely had time to think "Oh shit, I am about to die." I did think that, but something in my being was completely aware I was looking at a symbol, a response to my inner question. I felt immense awe and overpowering insight, but no fear. I knew I was face-to-face with my own nature.

Then I had another thought. "If this is what female power looks like, what is the image of male love and humility, the ability for men to be completely at their peak?" As soon as I had that thought, I found myself looking at and immersed in something quite different but equally magnificent, a lattice work of luminous golden light, like a web of facets in a diamond seen under a microscope. I saw a plane of connected squares of light with rounded, interlocked joints where each block of light connected. I gazed out at an endless field of diamond-like patterns. The crystalline image stretched on and on forever. It shone brilliantly, but there was no movement.

In Buddhist thought, there is a state of awareness called the diamond mind. I "knew" I was looking at the diamond mind. The lattice work of light was exactly as the Buddhist teacher had described it—a male's more compact, grid-like structure. It was luminous, exquisite, and boundless.

Then abruptly, I was back in my New York City foyer, standing next to my black travel suitcase, my wool coat draped over the handles.

I felt awe and gratitude. I knew that both visions—the tsunami as a symbol of boundless female power and the diamond facets as a symbol of refined male love and humility—were true.

Ever since that afternoon, this seeing has accompanied me. It's in my vision when I look at men and women, and sometimes it's in my meditation too. I think about the fact that yes, men have a more constrained, grid-like operating system—that is how life force flows through them—and its highest quality is realized through love and humility, the beautiful diamond mind.

And women have the ability for raw power to flow through them and take any shape or form, as they truly are the power species on the planet.

Women are the power gender—its highest form is the tsunami at full height—extremely, vibrantly, and exuberantly powerful.

Sometimes when I meditate, I do a visualization. I picture the roaring tsunami and enter into it, try to become it, and remember that my power level is that vast and expands into eternity. Women readers, please try this visualization when you meditate or just as a stand-alone practice during quiet time. This is who you are.

During meditation, men should visualize the exquisite diamond mind, a diamond lattice of light that goes on and on into eternity. This beautiful visualization will allow you to go very high and help you develop the innate love and humility that is your nature.

Of course, as pointed out by the young teacher many years ago, as you approach enlighten–ment, there is no gender energy difference. We all have the highest qualities of men and women inside of us. Men have that tsunami. Women have the diamond mind.

But along the path, for most of us, men need to cultivate and celebrate the diamond mind of love and humility. Women need to nurture, own, and express the incredible power of their tsunami nature.

4

POWER PARADIGMS FOR WOMEN

> Women, it turns out, are *built* to lead—
> particularly in the modern world.
>
> **—Helen Fisher**

As I sit on a bench in a small sea-facing park, I look out at a placid, still scene. I see water in a beautiful bay that's quite flat right now. There's very little wind. The waves are tiny ripples, barely visible. The deep turquoise water almost looks like glass. And yet if the force of any of these elements were to pick up—for example, the wind—then the wind will stir the waves. The waves will start to rise and crash to the shore with more force.

And let us say that the wind was accompanied by something like a high tide or possibly a surge from an event somewhere else in nature perhaps five hundred miles or several continents away, then what I would witness would be something much more forceful, possibly threatening to the shoreline here and capable of causing great damage.

This is the power of nature. Power events in nature display more rapid movement. In other words, when something is very, very calm and more contained, it's not that it lacks power but it is simply not a powerful manifestation; and when something is more fluid, more movement oriented, and characterized by rapid transmutation, then we say it is powerful.

Imagine you are looking at a wide sunlit snowbank on the side of a mountain. The slopes glisten, shiny and still. Suddenly, an unseen shift in the snowbank triggers an avalanche that rushes down a hill and loosens huge quantities of snow that explode down the hillside. The rapidity of the transformation generates huge amounts of power as snow and rocks cover everything in their path.

Consider an earthquake. Day after day, year after year, you live in a calm environment. All of a sudden, fault lines in the earth start to slip, releasing energy in waves that travel through the earth's crust, causing upheaval on the surface.

Think about hydroelectric power generation, torrents of water rushing through dams. If you have ever visited a dam, you observe the nature of movement and its inherent power as water activates specially designed turbines and roars and cascades out through chutes in the dam's wall.

Then think of wind gusts spinning windmills. Think about coal burning or nuclear fission. It's all about transmutation in as rapid a manner as possible.

In every case, what the generation of power has in common is the characteristic of increased fluidity, the ability for incrementally more rapid movement. Women, this is you!

Fluidity and changes is the primary characteristic of a female's energy body that surrounds and infuses her physical body. Life force, or *chi*, moves more rapidly through a woman's body. It's physical, too.

We menstruate every four weeks for about thirty-five years. Each menstruation cycle is complex, involving many different glands and hormones, and each cycle has separate phases that lead to a menstrual. This is complex and beautiful.

We are multi-orgasmic, and our orgasms engage more parts of the brain. We can bear children – with myriad pre-, during-, and post-physical changes – if we choose. If we choose, we lactate. We enter a menopause phase, opening new elements of power. Our inner power allows us to outlive men by many years.

All these physical traits represent power.

The subtle physical body of energy that surrounds a woman conducts energy much more rapidly than a man's subtle physical body. The life force of a woman is capable of much faster shifts and transmutations. That is the characteristic of power.

Yet all around you, you see women subjugating and squandering their power level, primarily to men. It's still an unspoken agreement--women are in some regard less powerful. This is a false agreement. I see it happening all the time—at home, in social gatherings, in the workplace.

Deep, embedded thoughts that women are somehow weaker than men are harmful to men and women. But these ideas have been held for so long that they continue to prevail—buried sexist views in both men and women. We know there are absurdist and confused views of women in most walks of life. Wrong or incomplete views of power lurk in women's hidden values and assumptions.

Even today I work with unmarried women in their thirties and forties still desperate to find husbands or life partners. In the meantime, they date men or women they barely like.

Why is it so necessary to find a male or female companion who, if you are "settling" for a less than stellar partner simply to have one, will hold down your power level? This means that you will not make the spiritual, emotional, financial, or intellectual gains you are capable of, all of which could be used to help others as well as yourself. Why? The answer is deep, old mental and emotional programming. There's no blame. Most people grow up with faulty role models. It's hard to aspire to be something you have not seen.

The result of not accepting your power level as a woman is imbalance.

Why do women who thrive in their careers, look sharp, and maintain physical fitness feel insecure? Why were the amazing ladies in Deepak Chopra's workshop studio feeling unconfident and incomplete?

There are several primary reasons: (1) they are misunderstanding the real nature of their power and the fact that they own it, (2) Deepak is a man, and most women subconsciously defer to men, and (3) they are not meditating too well yet.

What does meditation have to do with power? Isn't meditation turning inwards, becoming still and gaining peace? Yes, it is all of that, but please understand—inner stillness is not passive. It is dynamic and empowering. You feel clear and energized after meditation. Meditation helps you clear your mind of the embedded thoughts and feelings of inferiority that were and are passed to you in thousands of different ways. Meditation is the new power you bring to your life. It increases your fluidity and ability to cope in countless situations, whether you are male or female.

Deepak teaches meditation, but you are structured to meditate brilliantly.

Sometimes you will find yourself in a situation where your power is blocked. Who knows why? There may be ways around it, or it just may be time to retreat and put yourself in a different situation where there are no blockages and your power has an opportunity to rise.

The real, intense, and compelling power of women is hard for most men to accept, even if they acknowledge it verbally.

5

MEDITATION CLASS #1 — POWER

"Meditation" is one of those loaded words, like "power." Most people think they know what it is, but I assure you they do not know.

Meditation is a term that can create reactions of fear, revulsion, anxiety, antipathy, anticipation, hope, curiosity, or—worse—I know all about it already.

People, please erase your notions of meditation. What I call meditation is a way to increase the ability of your mind to *focus*. If you close your eyes right now, your mind is all over the map—thousands of thoughts race through your head. Your mind is never still. You are a prisoner of those thoughts; they grip and toss you like a surfer trapped under a large wave.

Learning to meditate, no matter what the technique, is always a way to get your mind to focus on one thing. Learning to focus intently is the way to emerge from that turbulent froth of thinking.

The one object of focus may be breath, a mantra (sound), a chakra (an energy center in your body), or a visualization. If you can focus your mind unwaveringly on one object and only that one object for increasing lengths of time, your mind can then let go of focusing on one thing and move naturally into pure stillness.

It makes sense. Your mind is filled with tons of thoughts. In meditation, you sit with your back straight, close your eyes (usually), and focus on a singular object. It's hard to do at first, but with time you get better at it. As you focus on that one thing, you can easily move from focusing on a singular point of attention to experiencing no thought whatsoever. You are now in the realm of all possibilities, your real self.

Why is this important for women? The most powerful states of mind are reached in inner stillness that is balanced with successful outer activity. As we begin to meditate, we experience the vast power within us, life force or chi.

There is more.

We women have been imprinted with so many incorrect views of self, our abilities, our roles. We women don't even see other women when we look at history books of the last few thousand years. Most written history is all about men. These imprints are silent reminders that women were repressed and pressured to accept a nonexistent role in history.

This is changing now. More women's history from all continents is starting to emerge. But the lack of historic acknowledgment is an imprint we carry. All the men we have known, all the women, our parents, grandparents, siblings, co-workers, school friends—they all have their own incomplete and erroneous ideas about the power of women, and we are still bombarded with these thoughts and impressions.

This has been going on for so long that we don't even know how repressed we are.

Think of it as tiny lines going into your body. From the time you were born, you have absorbed millions of mental and emotional impressions of infancy, girlhood, adolescence, and womanhood.

When you meditate, you don't have to analyze these lines. You stop thought and sweep them away. The lines are steadily expunged from your being.

All the restrictive thoughts, fears, assumptions, anxieties, insecurities are like clumps of seaweed and old fishing line clinging to the bottom of a boat. You don't need to examine every fleck of weed and ocean detritus on the hull. You lift the boat out of the water and sand it down until it's clean. When the hull is clean, the boat can operate at its intended speed and efficiency. That's what meditation is.

When you meditate, you won't necessarily know that a psyche scrub is taking place, but soon you will feel it. You will know it by your inner energy, calm, enthusiasm, and happiness. These feelings begin to bubble up to the surface of your being. That energized person is the meditating you. The one who can look at the algae, barnacles, and worms that built up on the boat bottom and know, "That's not me!" The one who can perform a mental sandblast. The one who can look others in the eye from a powerful place of meditative stillness and know, "This is me!"

How many times do you have to clean a boat's hull? It might be every two weeks, certainly right before a race, and daily if you have diving skills. Taking care of yourself with meditation is easier. To keep your head clean, it's best to meditate two times a day.

Meditation is about stopping thought. When you stop thought, the world stops and you experience your true being. The more stillness you have in your mind, the more you can discern all of life and gain happiness.

I would like readers of this book to have the cleanest mental, emotional, and spiritual vehicle they can achieve, and this is done through adding deep stillness back into your life.

There are many ways to meditate. In this book I describe three different meditation techniques that can be practiced individually or one after the other in a sequence.

The first technique, of course, is to meditate on power.

Power.

In martial arts, power is generated in the area of the solar plexus. The loud *kiai*, the warrior sound of the martial arts practitioner, comes from that area of the body.

Similarly, in yoga, there are seven main energy centers along the spine, and each is associated with a certain quality. Just below the navel is the power center. To feel where it is, put two fingers below your belly button and press lightly. Yup, that's where the power center is.

For your first meditation technique, I am going to ask you to find a comfortable place to sit in your home or office where you will not be disturbed. You can sit cross-legged or on a chair with your feet on the floor. The important thing is that your back is straight.

Close your eyes and focus on the area just below your navel. Feel free to keep your fingers lightly pressed there to help. When you focus, try to have no other thoughts in the mind. If helpful, you can visualize a bright golden-yellow orb of light there.

When thoughts come, and they will, when you become aware that you are thinking lots of thoughts, return your focus to that area just below your navel and try to keep your focus or gaze of the mind without thought in the power center of the body.

Do this for up to ten minutes. Do not be hard on yourself. This is not a contest. It's an exercise in feeling and stopping thought, and you will get better over time.

After ten minutes, slowly open your eyes and take a few deeper breaths. Don't engage in stressful activity right away. Take a bit of time to start going about your day.

Now that you've done this one time, next time try doing this same technique while listening to the first song on *Mandala of Light*, a beautiful meditation music CD by the band Zazen. You can download this music for free.

www.ramameditationsociety.org/mandala-light

By doing this meditation exercise two times per day, you will activate the power center in your body.

Other meditation techniques are presented throughout this book. As you learn them, alternating different meditation practices will help you build the strength of your mind and your meditative prowess.

6

LOVE AND HUMILITY FOR MEN

Sanskrit texts say that love is the essential force in the universe. This is true, and I once experienced it. This was back in the days when I was very involved with a meditation-focused spiritual group. The people and the practice meant everything to me. I went to Northern California to attend a course offered by that group, and I was turned away. I do not remember why, but it was probably because (though I did not know it then) my involvement with that group was winding down, and there also was a good dose of petty bureaucracy.

I was not allowed to participate in the course, and it hurt me to the core. I got on a bus and wept all the way back to my house in Southern California. Sobs, nonstop tears, and an endless slobbery nose engulfed me. My shoulders and chest heaved. My sadness was soul deep, and I couldn't get rid of it.

I entered the house and still felt so sad. That house had some crazy wallpaper, and I stared at it listlessly.

Suddenly, nothing was solid. Everything—walls, furniture, florid wallpaper, cabinets—became transparent and filled with waves of love. Everything was made of love. The waves were visual, gentle and persistent. The love was visceral. It washed over me and through me. A higher vibration of love. I couldn't believe it. The shag carpet, the leather couches, the black stair railings not solid. Everything was undulating with waves of love.

My tears dried. I observed the waves of love until they gently subsided and the house became solid again. I was comforted and humbled in the most amazing way.

When I speak of love as something men are innately good at realizing, I speak of this deep love. Not a flower-strewn, valentine-card love, but a deep ground state of love that underlies and holds life together, the golden grid that appeared as the symbol of a man's love.

Love and Humility for Men 43

Love of this type and humility are closely linked. Humility is not weakness—it comes from inner strength and a deep sense of worth and service. Gandhi changed the shape of an entire nation and world with his humility. The athletes we remember are not those who won the gold medal but those who won and were humble. They're the ones who stand out.

Humility has no shred of domination or control. It's a mindful approach to giving more to others than you take for yourself. We talk of a male ego. Humility is the non-macho self, the selfless person who loves and is happy and generous to the extent they can be. This type of humility is happy to think about because it's achievable, and yet it totally lightens the unemotional and false "be a man" notion that most men have overloaded on.

A false view of manliness has become deeply embedded in men's consciousness. It hurts men and the women they interact with.

Men, when I write that you are innately suited for love and humility—deep love for life and deep generosity of spirit—these are the traits I am writing about. Start somewhere and you will find you have a true knack for it.

Back in time, perhaps five thousand years ago, the loving nature of men was repressed, just as the innate power of women was repressed. There was an inversion of gender roles.

Now that women are realizing their own inner power and the unjust situation they have been subjected to, men can focus on what is truly suitable for them.

Visualize the golden grid of light resting on the white cloud. This is a vision of refinement, of love. Men's role is to move closer to that vision, just as women must return to their tsunami nature.

7

MEDITATION CLASS #2 — HEART

Hold out your right hand straight in front of you, then bring it back to your body, pointing your index finger to the center of your chest. Say "me." Touch the center of your chest. You have just located your heart center.

A few pages ago, you learned to meditate on your power center, one of the seven main nexuses of energy in the subtle physical energy body that surrounds your physical body. The Sanskrit term for these energy centers is "chakras." In the center of your chest is the heart center.

With your eyes closed, focus intently on the heart center. That means, direct your full mental focus to the center of the chest. You may visualize a glowing, luminous robin's egg blue orb there. As you focus and visualize this orb, try to have no other thoughts in your mind. When thoughts come, as soon as you realize you are thinking, return to your focus on the heart center and the robin's-egg blue orb of light as you gently push thought out of your mind.

Do this with eyes closed for ten minutes at first, then build up the time slowly to fifteen to thirty minutes. You can keep a watch or clock nearby and open one eye to see the time.

When you have finished meditating, slowly open the eyes. Take a few deeper breaths. Smile. It feels good to bow with gratitude to eternity.

You can also use the *Mandala of Light* music to meditate on the heart center. Now you can use two meditation techniques for one sitting. For the first song, follow the instructions for meditation on the power center. For the second song, follow the instructions for meditation on the heart center. It will be fun! You will discover a deeper, more ancient self that existed long before the inversion of gender roles and the suppression of women. You will uncover a shiny new self, capable of being, knowing, and accomplishing magnitudes more.

8

PEOPLE: SERENA WILLIAMS

Throughout this book, I highlight women who represent different aspects of power. Power is infinite. Naturally, it has many facets.

Serena Williams is arguably one of the world's greatest women's tennis players. She is one of the highest-paid athletes in the world. She loves sports, business, fashion, and now motherhood.

She became powerful by never giving up. She and her sister, Venus, began playing tennis at an early age, supported and encouraged by their father who homeschooled them until they reached high school.

Williams learned tennis from her father on the public courts in Los Angeles and turned professional in 1995, one year after Venus. The Williams family members were viewed as outsiders by the tennis community, but their skills attracted attention. Many predicted Venus would be the first Williams sister to win a Grand Slam singles title. It was Serena who accomplished the feat, winning the 1999 US Open. At that tournament the sisters won the doubles event, and over the course of their careers, the two teamed up for fourteen Grand Slam doubles titles.

Since that time, Serena has won twenty-three Grand Slams. She is known for her tenacity, her ability to rebound, her integrity, her determination to win. Her style and flair changed women's tennis from stuffy to exciting and cool.

What I love about Serena, and why I think she is a great example of the innate power of women, is her combination of hard work and authentic truth-telling.

To become successful, she trained all the time, even when she did not want to. She faced and overcame extreme self-doubt about her abilities and physical appearance. She worked incredibly hard. Whether she won or lost a game, she looked into herself again and again to assess the state of her being.

What would it do for your psyche if as a result of endless practice and guidance from strong coaches, you succeeded in perfecting a difficult tennis move, then you had to keep practicing it another thousand times?

You would learn about power, about sandblasting the bottom of your boat

Power looks flashy and exciting from the outside, but it is preceded by tremendous effort, discipline, and dedication.

Says Williams, "Luck has nothing to do with it, because I have spent many, many hours, countless hours, on the court working for my one moment in time, not knowing when it would come…

"With a defeat, when you lose, you get up, you make it better, you try again. That's what I do in life, when I get down, when I get sick, I don't want to just stop. I keep going and I try to do more. Everyone always says never give up but you really have to take that to heart and really do never definitely give up. Keep trying."

Williams wrote an article for the August 2019 issue of *Harper's Bazaar* in which she talks about pushing back against injustice when she sees it, about trying to change the world for her daughter, about the controversial 2018 US Open match against Naomi Osaka.

The essay illustrates what you can do when you become powerful (you can be heard), and what it takes to retain power – self truth.

In the final match against Osaka, Williams was issued three violations—the first for coach signaling, which Williams denies; the second for smashing her racket in frustration; and the third for calling the umpire a thief and demanding an apology. The violations probably caused her to lose the game.

After this public defeat, a losing moment for both Williams and Osaka, numerous journalistic debates ensued, with many sports writers maintaining that Williams had been treated unfairly. They compared her actions to years of far worse behavior by dozens of professional male tennis players engaging in highly public, serious infractions with little to no punitive consequences.

"In the end," Williams writes in *Harper's Bazaar*, "my opponent simply played better than me that day and ended up winning her first Grand Slam title. I could not have been happier for her."

Williams also writes that she struggled to recover from the loss and the surrounding controversy. She could not sleep. She sought therapy. She stopped playing tennis.

"This debacle ruined something that should have been amazing and historic," she said. "Not only was a game taken from me but a defining, triumphant moment was taken from another player, something she should remember as one of the happiest memories in her long and successful career. My heart broke. I started to think again, 'What could I have done better? Was I wrong to stand up? Why is it that when women get passionate, they're labeled emotional, crazy, and irrational, but when men do they're seen as passionate and strong?'"

She wrote an apology to Osaka. Osaka replied. Williams quotes her as writing, "People can misunderstand anger for strength because they can't differentiate between the two. No one has stood up for themselves the way you have and you need to continue trailblazing."

Ultimately, said Williams, "I felt defeated and disrespected by a sport that I love, one that I had dedicated my life to and that my family truly changed, not because we were welcomed, but because we wouldn't stop winning."

Williams never had power conferred on her. She discovered it, developed, and honed it. Williams' story is a realistic approach to women asserting their power level. You may not be welcomed, you may receive unfair pushback, but you will keep winning.

Williams expresses the force of the tsunami wave in action.

9

SEX MIX-UP

> And the day came when the risk to remain
> tight in a bud was more painful than the risk
> it took to blossom.
>
> —**Anaïs Nin**

Today we see more and more advocates for the removal of gender boundaries. Transgender, pangender, gender-fluid individuals are making their voices heard. Every stamp of human sexual identification is speaking out and demanding to be recognized without judgment or fear. This is admirable.

If you are transgender or gay, pangender, gender fluid, or metagender, just take the words in this book to heart and do the math. There is a high side to your sex. For women, it is power, and for men, it is profound, loving kindness.

Fact is, you will be miserable as hell if you are not yourself. If you as a person who identifies as a female think you are not a fortress of power, you will make myriad choices that will limit you and make you unhappy. If you as a person who identifies as a man think you are not a fortress of love and humility, you will also make choices that will blunt your ability to live a complete life.

Would you put your right foot into a left shoe and always walk that way? Would you put your clothes on backward and dress like that every day? Would you wear glasses meant for a blind person when you have outstanding vision? No, you would not do these things.

Yet today you as a woman or man do that. You wear a role that is not you. You wear a sense of yourself that was given to you by society and has been around for several thousand years. It is a false view, a left shoe on a right foot. The falsehood is best understood by going back to what we know about the most basic difference between male and female.

A man's subtle physical body or life force—or *kundalini*, as it is called in yoga—is denser, more tightly packed, more fixed, and it vibrates more slowly. A woman's subtle physical body is more pliant. It vibrates more quickly and is able to make tremendous changes and reshuffle itself constantly. This different essential quality of the two genders creates the ability for a man to naturally hold and contain many qualities of love and humility, and for a woman to express many qualities of power.

Over millennia, these roles have been completely switched. You see the role switch in your life, in the media, in the workplace. We still see that soft-hearted men are considered weak. Sometimes men are belittled by their own partners or wives for not being "alpha" enough. Powerful women are still considered "ball-breakers" and "bitches."

Some individuals and couples have instinctively rebelled against the role switch, but for the most part there is a deep-rooted compromise on the part of women to appear even a little less powerful than the men (or same sex partners) they are with. It's an unspoken agreement. It's not a good agreement. It's a seriously crappy agreement.

As Virginia Woolf wrote in *A Room of One's Own*, "Women have served all these centuries as looking glasses possessing the magic and delicious power of reflecting the figure of man at twice its natural size."

When I commuted every day from the suburbs of Westchester, NY, into Grand Central Station in Manhattan, I often sat next to a woman who was a successful lawyer. At one point her firm offered her a position that was a big career advancement—she would be a lead partner with the ability to influence many of the firm's decisions. It was a logical step up for her. We discussed her feelings about taking the position.

Her kids were almost grown up, her husband was also a lawyer, but he was not getting the same level of recognition. She felt that if she took that role, it would upset the balance of power in their relationship. She would have considerably more prestige in her job than her husband. She felt it would be a problem for their marriage. She did not take the promotion.

I thought her decision was backward. She was presented with a doorway to increase her power level, and she could bring her innate ability to deal with power to the new position. In this case, fearing her husband's insecurity held her back. She did not give her husband the opportunity to recognize that her innate quality, her role, her destiny was to lead, and for her not to do that was to hurt herself and future generations of men and women.

It doesn't have to be this way. One of my friends, who holds a powerful position in US state government, says, "All the conferences I go to and the authority I hold give my husband bragging rights. He loves it."

One of my business colleagues has a twelve-year-old daughter, Julie, who used to be a math whiz. But as early as age ten, as Julie entered her tween years, she pushed away from math. Math became uncool to her and her girl peers because excelling at math was something boys do rather than girls. She did not want to compete and appear "unfeminine." My friend could not get her daughter to embrace math again.

This preteen cultural conditioning is backward. Mental prowess is empowering. The STEM (science, technology, engineering, and math) studies build up a girl's self-confidence by challenging her mind. People think society has changed, but when girls lower their educational levels at age nine or ten to be behind the boys, when preteen and teenage girls try to make themselves less powerful in order to attract boys, they are setting in motion a pattern that will follow and harm them for decades.

Instead of powering down in their tweens and teens, an age when girls' healthy subtle physical bodies are most luminous, the tweens and teens are a perfect time for girls to power up. Girls should feel comfortable about making decisions that will empower them for the rest of their lives.

There are so many examples of the gender mix-up. Across the globe, entire nations repress women in horrific and humiliating ways. Women earn less than men for the same job. Women are not promoted to the leadership positions they deserve because of inaccurate perceptions about their ability to handle power. While the situation is improving, a lack of female leadership still prevails in politics, religion, science, academia, business, and media. It reflects a poverty of recognition of a woman's innate ability to express and exemplify power.

Female power and male love and humility are worth sitting down to discuss. One of the reasons for the gender flip-flop is that men often do not understand that the very thing—powerful women—that seems so threatening to them is not threatening at all.

If you know the grass is green in the spring, it doesn't threaten you. If you know the sky is blue when it's a lovely day, it does not threaten you. If men understand that the innate quality of women is power and that their own innate quality is love and humility, there is no fear. These are amazing and exciting paths to explore and pursue.

Women also need to give space to men to be loving and humble. A man may wonder, If I'm going to explore how much love I can feel for life, will the partner in my life accept it? Will I be seen as a wimp if I do not dominate and control? It's a sea change of roles.

"After I heard the teachings on women and power," my friend Lorraine told me, "I took my husband out for a date night so we could have a good talk. I said I knew I was powerful but sometimes held back in case he would feel threatened. I said I didn't want to hold back anymore. I also said I saw how loving and gentle he is, and I wanted him to know that he could go a lot farther in that direction and it would be fine with me. For our marriage, it was a healing and transformative discussion. It took pressure off both of us and changed us for the better."

Many women look to their partners to be stronger than they are, not too macho but somewhat macho. They flatter their partners by making them the final decision makers and pack leaders. Women need to examine these ideas in terms of realizing their healthy natural power. If a woman is acting less powerful than her male partner, she is lowering her power level considerably. Think of a huge tsunami trying to fit into a grid.

If a woman is attracted to a person with anger or hypermasculine machismo, then she's spending time in the presence of someone who swaggers, who will not be courteous and feeling, who will not be responsible. If a woman accepts hypermachismo in her life or accepts sexual violence as normal or even desirable (e.g., the wrong man or partner), she is choosing to drain her own power.

Perhaps she thinks she should not be as powerful as she knows herself to be. This pulls in Mr. or Ms. Wrong. Sex mix-up! Even worse, you are harming your energy body.

Anger and negative emotions harm a woman's subtle physical body more than a man's. Too much anger directed toward her will make a woman physically sick. This is because that luminous, rapidly moving energy body that extends out around a woman's physical body is highly sensitive to negative thoughts and feelings, even the subliminal ones.

A man's more compact energy body can absorb the energy of anger and violence with less damage.

There are no meek and docile women. There are no macho men. Just lots of great pretenders.

Ultimately, getting inherent gender qualities right—whether gay, fluid, trans, or straight—is about being happy, healthy, and fulfilled. If men and women express basic sex qualities—female as an expression of vast power and male as an expression of infinite love and humility—the planet will become balanced and households will become balanced. The violence we see in society will diminish.

10

PEOPLE: MALALA YOUSAFZAI

> When the whole world is silent, even one voice becomes powerful.
>
> —**Malala Yousafzai**

Malala is the young woman who as a girl was shot in the head by Taliban barbarians because she wrote a blog supporting the right of girls to attend school in her native Pakistan.

As she told Ellen DeGeneres, the Taliban made a mistake. Because instead of stopping her, she lost her fear of being attacked and realized that nothing could stop her from exposing the situation many young women face in obtaining an education.

Malala speaks of education as her Western peers might speak of a new car or a great vacation. She is in love with education. When she heard she won a Nobel Peace Prize, she was in the middle of her school day. She refused to leave her classes to speak to the press. She insisted on completing her schooling that day because it meant more to her to receive an education than to talk to the press about an award.

Power-raiser—education. Malala orates on this topic, and she is right. Education provides mental strength, perspective, and the ability to maneuver in the world. The mind is a muscle, and education exercises the mind and makes it more powerful. The Buddhist teacher I studied with said, "You can never be too rich or too educated." We'll discuss the rich part in another chapter, but let's focus on education.

In Pakistan, where Malala grew up and where her father founded and ran several schools, a secular education is prized as the way to lead a successful life, to break through the barriers of geography and physical circumstances. In Pakistan, an education is not every young woman's right. In practice, it is a hard-fought path that is prized and considered the best good fortune.

Before she was shot, as a young spokesperson for female education, Malala broke barriers that surround all women.

Even in the West, education for women is relatively recent. In 1956, Ruth Bader-Ginsburg was one of only 8 women amid 492 men entering Harvard Law School.

Let's imagine that you are a man and you are threatened by the power of women. You feel intuitively that education creates a higher and more integrated level of personal power in men, and you don't want the same thing to happen to women. So you block it. It is the classic tendency in human nature to try to destroy what one is threatened by.

Any religion or society that justifies denying education or offering lesser-quality education to women is in the throes of the worst male oppression.

Of course, the power species should be educated, which is still not the case in much of the world. Malala continues to work very hard, remaining very focused, staying extremely persistent to make her point—women deserve and must, for the benefit of society, receive not only a good education but the best education available.

Malala is an example of the power of women. People feel her inner power, they feel her intelligent mind, her courage, and they support her personal breakthroughs because her success helps everyone in many ways.

Courage and bravery are gender free. Hard work and persistence are gender free. Women, when they display these innate qualities, as Malala is now doing, help end millennia of gender misperceptions.

11

MEDITATION CLASS #3 — INTELLECT

The intellect.

Touch the center of your forehead. In Eastern philosophy, this point is considered the center of knowledge, perception, and mental acuity. It is another energy center, or chakra, in the subtle physical body.

Close your eyes and for several minutes, focus your attention on the center of your forehead. Picture a round orb of luminous white light in the center of your forehead. Try to have no other thoughts in your mind but instead focus intently. And when thoughts do come into your mind, as soon as you realize you are no longer focusing on the luminous white orb in the center of your forehead, return your focus to that area and visualization.

Do this for five to ten minutes. When you are done, fold your hands together and bow, just to thank the universe. Feel gratitude. Take a few deeper breaths. Very slowly open your eyes.

If you are using the *Mandala of Light* album as part of your meditation practice, focus on the navel center/power chakra for the first song, on the heart center/heart chakra for the second song, and on the intellect center for the third song. If you have time to meditate for a longer period of time, try this sequence for two songs apiece. Now you are an adventurer in worlds of light.

12

SEX MISTAKES

> Learn from the mistakes of others. You can't live long enough to make them all yourself.
>
> **—Eleanor Roosevelt**

From root cause—the embedded sex role switch—to overt misogyny, there are destructive sex mistakes operative in our world, some of which are tragic and preventable. Here's a partial list, assembled mainly to demonstrate how deeply sex mistakes permeate our lives.

1. Objectification of women

When through a rock video, movie, fashion show, video game, magazine cover, or social media advertisement, a woman is treated as a blank, dangerous, or vacant sexual object—imagery that effectively takes the innate power of women and jerks it around, turns it sideways, and perverts it— people still pick up on the sexual energy, but it registers dark, not bright.

Perhaps you're in the supermarket checkout line. You see a glossy magazine cover with a photo of a woman's full, partially open bright red lips and her tongue out. The image projects a sense of sexuality and lust, and it uses the power of women in a fractured and unfriendly way. Every person who sees that magazine cover has to react, to either agree, disagree, or ignore. The image exploits the power of women and resents it at the same time. Rather than instilling admiration, these images of women's body parts sow seeds of anger, violence, and mistrust. The distortion is another trope that women have to push back against.

All those pouting images of women on social media? Pouting is for children, not women. When adult women pout into their selfies, what are they saying? Asked differently, does pouting demonstrate independence, strength, and character?

Recently, I spoke with a thirty-two-year-old friend whom I have known for many years. He is a nice-looking, smart, meditating Buddhist man.

I asked him what stands in the way of women being recognized as powerful beings by men, and he gave me a one-word answer, "pornography." Yeah, I was surprised. He said that I probably did not realize how many men use pornographic videos for sexual arousal and that he himself had become a porn addict at age ten. It had taken him two unhappy decades to overcome it.

After we spoke, I wept because my friend had to go through something so antithetical to his being. I researched pornography addiction online. In this book, I will not go into the lengthy research on this topic. You can Google "effect of pornography on the brain," and it's all there—the link to violence against women and families, the rising use of internet pornography by men and women in all age groups, the true chemical addiction, the increasingly degraded views of sex partners and oneself, the rise of sexual dysfunction. If you think the issue has not been a problem for you, people in your family, or people you know at work, this may not be the case. Please Google and become informed.

Today as I write, due to easy online availability and peer group pressure, young men and women are exposed to an outpouring of porn. There is nothing wrong with sexuality. It is a beautiful and powerful spiritual force. Sexuality when abused has the opposite effect: it is draining and dys–functional. Porn supports the abuse of women and destructive mental tendencies. So add it to the hull-scrubbing. It should not be in your or your partner's life – if you are interested in gaining power.

2. Women believing that their main power is sexual attractiveness

Sensuality is a strong power of women, but it's just part of your power spectrum. Sexual attractiveness as a way of life blooms during our teen years and can last well into the fifties or beyond.

Fine, lady friends, but it's 1,000 percent better to have a good profession. The sexual energy you attract will be filled with the rough, violent energy that many men project toward women. As a naturally psychic perceiver, you will be negatively affected by this rough energy. Over time, you will be drained and worn down by this low-grade attention.

Sexual power is a no-brainer for women. Part of that fluid subtle physical body that surrounds a woman can be used to radiate waves of sexual energy and direct it to others, and women do this much more easily than men.

Do you want men to regard you as the sexiest woman in the room? Let's look at it another way. Do you want to weaken your subtle physical body? Do you want to lose your self-confidence? Do you want to repeatedly make bad decisions for your well-being? If so, go for grabbing sexual attention. It's a cheap short-term win—easy for a woman to do—but it carries a long-term cost. A damaged subtle physical body leads to illness (mental, emotional, and physical) and a low energy level.

Save the sexual energy waves and flares for someone you love, who reciprocates your love.

A story: My colleague Lucy is an independent, single, happy professional woman who earns a six-figure income in technology. Back in her twenties, when she first embarked on a technical career, her family—particularly her prettier, sexier older sister who had married a wealthy man—thought she was eccentric and misguided to go into technology.

Twenty years later, the older sister is divorced and broke, has no marketable skills, and praises Lucy every day for choosing a path of economic and emotional independence. The cute sex-kitten thing didn't last for my friend's sister. Technology and self-sufficiency worked out brilliantly.

Remember that for thousands of years women could not support themselves. They had to depend on men. Now women can lead independent lives in many countries. The strategic selection process about how to earn a living and what to do should begin at a young age for girls and can start at any time for women.

3. Men holding a limited view of women

To maintain a degraded view of women, to feel superior, dominant, angry, or threatened because a woman has a more fluid, powerful nature and a higher sexual capacity creates a lower state of consciousness. A man who seeks to be fulfilled in his life should drop these feelings and instead seek to respect, honor, and nurture the power of women. Similarly, women should respect, honor, and nurture love and humility in men.

The wrong ideas that men have been brought up with—any hint of male superiority—is a personality trait that leads to imbalance and inner anger. Everyone has both male and female inside them. Why hate or fear a part of yourself?

One of my male colleagues explained to me that he had been brought up to repress his emotional feelings. They were viewed by his peers and family as "girly" (there we go again, that term as a pejorative) and weak. When he was exposed to the metaphysical teachings on the innate love and humility of men, he decided to consciously try feeling love for small things first. He chose his car, houseplants, and wild birds since there were many around his house.

"It started with those three simple things," he said. "I had to practice, to remind myself to feel heart-love feelings, and it wasn't easy. But after a while, I really did feel love, and it expanded throughout my life. It's a joyful, liberating feeling now, and I'm no longer afraid of love. It's me!"

4. Media misrepresentation of women

There's an excellent film on this topic. It's called *Miss Representation*.[1] The film is a few years old now, but the topic is still on target. The film chronicles consistent misrepresentation of women in film, media, politics, classrooms, and

---

[1] *Miss Represention*, 2011, director Jennifer Siebel Newsom

boardrooms, which spread false views of women throughout society. If we fail to acknowledge the power of women, the next generation of girls and women is short changed. As Marian Wright Edelman said, "You can't be what you can't see."

As more women gain positions of power in the entertainment industry, we are seeing a much broader spectrum of women in more powerful roles. Strong female heroines and supporting characters are more common. But there's still that undercurrent—women chase men as if they were trophies, and they struggle to find or express their inner strength.

The tide is starting to shift, but the überpowerful woman, the enlightened woman with her energy and power fully risen is still rare.

Men's domination of the media – the illustrative Harvey Weinstein debacle – is starting to recede, but statistics show that women are still in the minority.

How can the power species be in the minority? It is wrong.

The #metoo movement in which thousands of women continue to come forward to say they were sexually abused by bosses, or by powerful figures in their profession or sport demonstrates progress for the rights and unification of women. The huge number of incidents that generated this movement is horrific but real.

Ladies, we are emerging from thousands of years of intolerable and imbalanced behavior. There is no superior gender. Men and women are *not* the same, it is true. Women are more powerful.

5. Women using their power to manipulate

For millennia, the only way a woman could be successful in life was through marriage. Sure, there was the occasional Queen Elizabeth I. But usually, there was no choice but marriage. You'd grow up and you'd marry, and the quality of your life was completely determined by the man you married. This is still true today in many nations.

So what would an innately powerful woman do, knowing her only chance at a decent life was to land the right guy? "Catching a man," "landing a man," "hooking a man," "snagging a man" are still prevalent phrases. Entire reality shows and internet dating services are based on this moth-eaten concept.

In history, here's what women did. Women have a powerful ability to use their luminous energy field to affect and change the attention of other people. They can do this much more readily than a man. One of the ways that women have traditionally overcome their repression is to use that skill to send out their powerful sexual energy to convince a man into thinking he is interested in her. This is very doable. Women and girls do it all the time.

The problem is that this is a form of manipulation. As long as women exist in a society where they are being viewed as a commodity and have no escape route except to throw out a net of sexual energy, along with images and ideas that they think will capture, hook, snag, or land a man, their actions are understandable. But now that's not the case, certainly not in most of Western society. Women shouldn't feel that manipulating men into being attracted to them is what they ought to be doing with their power.

To manipulate a man to desire you with that fluid subtle body you have is not a good use of it. It's the consciousness of manipulation, and if you are in that consciousness, it will not make you happy. Plus, once the spell wears off and the partner you have "snared" or "netted" discovers how powerful you are, the response may be more dire than you anticipated.

I spoke with a male real estate agent who is on his third marriage. He laments that in both of his first two marriages, the women changed completely after he married them, and he felt compelled, in spite of economic loss and legal unpleasantness, to divorce each woman. Turned out he thought he married "innocent, sweet, girlish" women, and after the marriage, they behaved more like the powerful adults they always were.

OK, lady friends, we know the innocent, girlish thing is a ploy. You are a tsunami, risen. My real estate colleague fell for an act, and when the women involved felt safe about changing the act to reflect more reality, he divorced them. Manipulation, false and unrealistic ideas of women—it's a lose-lose situation.

6. Women being unsupportive of other women

In the past, landing that right man was a zero-sum game. If you had to harm your own sister, you did whatever it took to snare the man who would ensure your well-being and your children's well-being.

That game is over. Teamwork, sisterhood, helping other girls and women succeed, mentoring, inspiring—this is the game that is happening and fun.

Most women were not raised to experience sisterhood. Perhaps it would have been too empowering? A whole group of bonded women? Today women need to be aware of deep background programming that promotes distrust or dishonor of fellow women so that they can completely overthrow it. When I see photos now of women who get together to promote causes, solve planetary issues, or discuss challenges facing women, I see the power of a tsunami wave at work.

A large wave is not one wave. It is composed of many waves. This is why surfers experience bumps as they ride down the surface of a large wave – they are surfing many waves combined into one. Similarly, it is natural for women with their fluid energy to express greater insight, faster decision-making, honor, camaraderie, respect, and trust.

Today women gather in "posses" to go out and party, but dig deeper and you find out that the posse is a placeholder until these same ladies find "the right man."

When shared actively and supportively, however, whether in a posse, a sports team, or a boardroom, the high-power level among women is a dynamic creative force unto itself.

Women supporting other women is a huge differentiator. In a recent US budget crisis, photos were taken of older, white male politicians glaring grimly at each other with fixed jaws, ideas, and patterns. At the same time, images appeared of a group of bi-partisan, multiracial women who met to discuss the budget crisis. While the men were so immovable and rigid they nearly pushed the nation over the edge, the women jointly agreed that they could end the crisis in weeks if not days. Why? Because when smart, educated, and hardworking women share power, the result is far greater than any one individual in the room.

Intelligent fluidity emerges. Boundaries dissolve quickly. The tsunami starts to reach its full height.

"There is a special place in hell for women who don't help other women."

—Madeleine Albright

7. Paying women less for the same work, failure to promote women

Oh, c'mon now! Any corporation or agency that knowingly pays women less for the same work is engaged in duplicity and lies. Today women still make up a small fraction of top leadership in business. There are few women billionaires and many male billionaires. Since women are adept at power in all its forms, this is a major issue in the competitive marketplace and a roadblock to long-lasting success.

Many women in the middle layers of management are grateful for their progress and fearful of making waves. But if you look around your workplace and see a total gender imbalance in pay scales and management leadership, you must do yourself and your workplace a great favor by taking visible, practical steps to correct the error and achieve balance.

Books abound on negotiating skills, management skills, everything you as a fast-learning woman need in order to get the same or more money than your male colleagues. Sometimes it means overcom–ing the fear of asking for a raise. Wait a minute! Why do you even have that fear? Who is the tsunami here?

8. Physical violence against women

We read daily headlines of women's corpses found and male acquaintances or partners arrested for the crime.

Rapes, beatings, child marriages, genital mutilation, women kidnapped and forced into prostitution – these are just some of the horrific crimes against women that are perpetuated and even tolerated in some parts of our global village. These are symptoms of men so warped and threatened by the power of women that they try to destroy it in violent ways. The reverberations of these crimes are heinous.

The oppression and suppression of women *is* the source of world violence. The young Buddhist teacher saw that in the 1980s. Now data proves it. The impeccably well-researched book *Sex and World Peace*,[2] reports on findings that the most violent nations in the world are the ones where violence against women is most endemic. Data collected over ten years demonstrates an undeniable relation-

---

[2] *Sex and World Peace*, Valerie M. Hudson, Bonnie Ballif-Spanvill, Mary Caprioli, Chad F. Emmett, 2012, Colombia University Press

ship between the treatment of women in everyday life and a nation's propensity for engaging in war. The authors maintain that the best indicator and predictor of a nation's ability to achieve peace is not the type of government, wealth, military expenditures, or religion. The best predictor is how well its girls and women are treated.

This project continues to track and display up-to-the-minute data on women's welfare, and maps the global regions where women are not safe (most of the world). You can join this mail list for updates:

www.womanstats.org

Women who are able to achieve and exert their natural power create conditions conducive to peace. Violence and the repression of women create continual war and disharmony.

Every empowered woman helps all men and women succeed.

In today's violent world, women must increase their discernment and act on their intuition if there are warning signs of violence.

It is critical that men overcome their millennia of repression of their golden grid-like nature.

As long as gender imbalance and confusion exist, the planet remains violent and ecologically ruined.

13

PEOPLE: ZHOU QUNFEI

> I think it's important not to get carried away when you are successful—and not to let yourself feel gloomy when times are bad.
>
> —Zhou Qunfei

One of the only self-made female billionaires in the world, Zhou Qunfei was born on a farm in China.[3]

As a girl, she raised pigs and ducks. Her mother died when she was five, and her father was blinded in an industrial accident when she was eight years old. In spite of her family life, Zhou Qunfei excelled at school, and at age fifteen, she

---

[3] The story of Zhou Qunfei is based on numerous online articles about her life and work.

moved to a nearby city to earn a living. She got a job in a factory, learned lens making, and opened her own factory.

Over the next decade, Zhou built up her new lens-making factory. The factory soon employed over one thousand people and drew the interest of Motorola in 2003.

A ruthless competitor tried to steal the contract from her. She reached out to Motorola, explained the situation, and got their support to continue. Zhou had learned a lesson she never forgot: perseverance creates success.

After the Motorola deal, Zhou expanded her client base to other mobile phone makers, including Nokia, Samsung, and Apple. With Apple as a client, her company became the dominant supplier of lens technology in China.

Expanding a business quickly is challenging for all entrepreneurs, and Zhou often used her personal resources to finance new plants.

Managing and attracting top resources to a business is also a considerable challenge. Many years and tens of thousands of employees later, she took twenty of her senior executives on a team-building trip to climb a five-thousand-foot mountain. About halfway up, some of them wanted to turn around, but Zhou would not let them.

"Because when you give up halfway," she told CNBC, "you won't have the courage to come back and start from the bottom all over again. Only when we persist, can we succeed. Don't give up because of a little setback."

Reports state that Zhou designs and oversees nearly every step of the manufacturing process, a detail-oriented approach she traces to her childhood. "My father had lost his eyesight," she told CNBC. "So if we placed something somewhere, it had to be in the right spot, exactly, or something could go wrong," she said. "That's the attention to detail I demand at the workplace." She says another secret to her success is the desire to learn.

In March 2015, Zhou's Lens Technology went public, and today the company is valued at $11.4 billion and has over 90,000 employees in 32 factories.

As an expression of female power, Zhou Qunfei demonstrates hard work, persistence, ingenuity, teamwork, mental acuity, and confidence when it matters. When someone called her with the opportunity of a lifetime, she did not say "Yes, but…" or "Yes, I hope so." She said yes. A doorway opened, and she walked through it. Then she fought hard and successfully to maintain momentum and change.

Zhou shuns media attention, and that is fine, too. Remember that sensitive subtle physical body you have? Do you want to be famous and have millions of people thinking about you? Probably not. Instead, use the power you have as a woman to become successful in your chosen endeavor, and then you can help others along the way. You become a template for success.

14

THE SEX KOAN

> Be strong, believe in freedom and in God, love yourself, understand your sexuality, have a sense of humor, masturbate, don't judge people by their religion, color or sexual habits, love life and your family.
>
> **—Madonna**

A *koan* is a Zen Buddhist term. It refers to a phrase or an image or a moment in time that so radically shifts your awareness that you see things in a new, brighter, and more truthful way.

Zen Buddhists use koans to teach about reality.

The koan of sex starts at an early age, when we become interested in and gear our lives toward sexuality. We usually identify our sexual orientation early in life. Sexuality is a driving force at earlier and earlier ages because today's children are exposed to so much sexuality in television, film, video games, shopping malls, magazines, music videos, TV, online almost everything.

Sex is fine, heterosexuality is fine, homosexuality is fine, transgender is fine, metasexuality, pansexuality—all fine. There is no spiritual, moral, ethical, or other problem with gender identities.

While there is no problem with having sex with a consenting, loving, and supportive partner of any stripe, there are high-impact problems with having sex with Mr. or Ms. Wrong, a.k.a. Mr. or Ms. Depressed, Destructive, Angry, Jealous, Insecure, Judgmental, Greedy, Selfish, Emotionally Cold... You know.

Sex with Mr. or Ms. Wrong is particularly problematic for women. As we know, during sex, women tend to open their hearts and emotions. For many women, the positive experience of physical intimacy is this natural openness to complex emotional and sexual pleasures.

Research conducted in 2011 took MRI brain scans of women having orgasms and found that the fluidity and power of the female orgasm activates many more parts of the brain, including more emotional centers, than a male orgasm.[4]

Researchers at the University of Michigan Health System found that emotional well-being plays a bigger role in a woman's drive for sex than in a man's.[5]

Emotions augment the physical experience of sex for women. Yet that very openness means you are receptive to the mind state of the person you are with. You may just think you are opening your legs during sex, ladies, but during sex you are *this close* to the energy body of your sexual partner. You are opening your *being* to your partner.

If during sex you are with a person who harbors any negative or limiting feelings about you; if that person has any limiting or negative views of women in general; if you are with a person who is threatened by the power of women; if he or she is in any way subtly threatened by the sexual power

---

[4] Szalavitz, Maia. "First 3D Movie of Orgasm in the Female Brain," Dec. 01, 2011, Time *Magazine*, http:/healthland.time.com/2011/12/01/first-3d-movie-of-orgasm-in-the-female-brain/

[5] Christensen, Jen, "Women's Desire for Sex is Complicated, Not Strictly Hormonal, Study Finds," November 21, 2014, CNN.com

of women; if he has been brought up to believe, incorrectly, that he is the person with power; if he believes he is supposed to be dominating, particularly during sex, then because of your emotional receptivity, those feelings will enter into you during sex. (Note that whatever your gender identity, these observations apply to the person who is your fleeting or long-term sexual partner.)

If during the time you are making love, your partner is in performance mode and consciously or subconsciously thinking "I have to be more powerful than my partner," your partner is already in the wrong state of mind. She or he is not in a state of love and giving. She or he's in a state of domination. If as part of your openness, you accept this emotion, your energy will be drained. Limiting, dominating mind states are extremely jarring and harmful to your powerful but sensitive subtle physical body, the luminous energy body of a woman.

Many women have experienced this.

One woman I know told me that when she first had sex and lost her virginity, she felt she had been run over by a Mack truck. She felt it took her years to recover from it. But because of her mental conditioning, she thought that was supposed to happen, that somehow her self-esteem was supposed to plummet. She was thrown off her path for years just by having teenage sex with a man who didn't care about her, and afterward, with men who did not esteem her at all. They thought of her as someone fluffy, disposable, not to be taken seriously. They did not see her as powerful. She began to think of herself in the same way and acted accordingly.

What really happened when my friend first had sex? When a man who viewed her as a disposable young bimbo entered her body, which is when the two subtle physical bodies are the most united and close, she got drained, not only of her energy but of her self-confidence and self-esteem. She thought this was normal and allowed it to happen over and over again for many years.

You have to make sure, ladies, that the man (or woman) being allowed into your body is only projecting into you the highest views of your power and your being. And that will be the partner who honors the highest ideal of power in you, the tsunami fully risen. If a partner can't accept that about you, the woman they are with, then he or she is doing you a great disservice. Because those thoughts are literally entering you during sex. Their lower opinion of you is literally thrown into your open being, and you will think they are your own.

In order to attain the powerful, higher, clear, and happy states of mind that we all seek and have a natural ability to achieve, in order to progress along life's path and experience your highest attainments in career, finances, leadership, emotional growth, spiritual growth, and education, you want to have all your power.

It's necessary for women to begin to reclaim their power at the most essential level of being. It does not by any means necessitate a complete breakdown between sexual partners, but it does mean that we as women must become more conscious of the energy transpositions between ourselves and the sexual partners in our lives.

Consider the confusion level of young men. They've been handed so many false images of themselves and women, sometimes from infancy. Even if they have a mom who is successful, what about video games, what about advertising, what about films? What about the adults hovering over the baby's crib cooing "cute little" at a girl and "big handsome" at a boy?

It must be so confusing for boys to see degrading images of women from a young age and then to have to grow up with a wrong view. For young men to be coached to suppress love and humility, even though those are their innate and powerful male qualities, throws boys growing into adulthood off their paths. Most men have had terrible upbringings, with "manness" rewarded and "girlness" feared.

In the sex koan, men have as many layers of the onion to unpeel as women.

What's a woman to do? Sex can be wonderful and beautiful. You do not have to be celibate. What you have to do is be careful choosing a partner. And if you have a partner who has been raised with wrong views of women, then it's very good to discuss this topic with them. Tell them about the energetic difference between men and women, that women represent power, that negativity toward women hurts the planet, not just you.

And allow them to be who they are. Let them be loving, not just toward you but toward life. If that happens, men and women will both feel like they moved out of a tight, splintery box and into a sea of possibilities. Both sexes will gain energy. Women will feel a fabulous energy gain simply by removing many of the negative factors that they have unknowingly allowed into their lives.

This is when meditation becomes so helpful. If both partners in a relationship meditate, they are both discovering deeper parts of their being that are powerful and loving. They are capable of sharing a more refined love with each other as they continue to meditate.

One of the nicest things that couples can do for each other is for both (not just one) to learn to meditate and practice regularly, every day. Within weeks, a new quality of love will surface that will make sexuality more profound and loving. How beautiful to becoming open to the higher ranges of someone else's spiritual nature, feelings brought about through meditation.

When I see confident young female teens suddenly looking insecure and drained, I intuit it's because—in a girl's curiosity and eagerness to check out sexuality—they had sex with someone who really did not care about them, thought low thoughts not only of them but of women in general, and whose own love and humility were probably very stunted. Instead of growing powerful and strong during adolescence, these girls block their power level and growth by absorbing the negative energy of others during sex.

It's not worth it. Teens and preteens, wait until you find somebody nice to have sex with. Don't be so eager to have sex that you're going to have it with someone who has a low view of women (and probably of themselves). Those ideas are going to slam into you like that Mack truck, and you will think the ideas are your own. It's a psychic transfer, subtle but powerful.

You don't have to have sex all the time. Celibacy is nice, too. You have choices. Spending time by yourself is also wonderful.

All these realizations are important for a person who wants to be independent. You have to realize that there's a wrong operating system called innate anger and a repressive attitude toward women that many, many people have—primarily men—because they were raised with it. Can they let go of that attitude? Yes, of course, if they want to. It's called "neural plasticity"—you can change your attitudes.

Men, you should feel relieved and joyful to know that your innate qualities of love and humility will be recognized and valued by women. This is a two-way street.

We're not blaming anyone. What we are saying, ladies, is that it's important to get your own balance back, get your own being back, get your own self back. You are a deeply powerful woman. Even if you have never felt powerful, by cutting out the negative influences in your life (you know what they are), becoming aware and proud of your fluidity, and observing what is going on, your power level will rise.

Sex can be a beautiful, powerful, high transposition of consciousness. This is described in the literature on tantric sexuality. Every woman is psychic. Ask yourself if your sexual partner is adding to your energy or decreasing it. Sometimes change happens instantly. Other times it happens more slowly.

> (S)he who controls others
> —May be powerful,
> But (s)he who has mastered herself
> —Is mightier still.
>
> —Lao Tzu

15

MEDITATION CLASS #4 — HINTS AND TIPS

Meditation is simple. Meditation is about learning to focus on one thing (a visual object, a sound, an energy center in your subtle physical body, for example) in order to let go into stillness. There isn't one way to meditate. There are many ways, and it's good to know several ways so that if you're stuck in one form of practice, you can try others.

One key advice I will give you is about thoughts during meditation. You are trying to intently focus on one thing, but thoughts still gallop into the mind. Thoughts are not "release of stress." Thoughts just mean you are in the early stages of meditation, before you can easily focus your mind and move into no-thought or stillness.

Thoughts during meditation do not have more significance than other thoughts. If you find you are having angry thoughts or you are thinking about another person during the whole meditation period, then stop meditating. Open your eyes for a few moments and break the chain.

Thinking about someone during meditation brings your attention right next to theirs. You are sensitive during meditation. You don't want to touch and draw into your being the energy of another person. So be mindful during meditation and don't worry if you need to open your eyes for several seconds to cut a negative train of thought. Your goal is to still your mind.

Here are ideas to make your practice more fun and exceptional.

1. Listen to music while meditating. I recommend Zazen music and recommend Zazen's *Enlightenment* for starters. The resonance of meditation pervades this music. *Canyons of Light* is a magical set of songs for late afternoon meditation. Select more free music from www.ramameditationsociety.org/resources/type/music

2. Chant a mantra aloud at the start of your meditation. Close your eyes and chant the

mantra *SRING* aloud seven times. Elongate the sound, especially the middle part. Something like *sriiiiiinnng*. *SRING* is a mantra of beauty and abundance. Once you have finished chanting, begin one of your focusing exercises from class 1, 2 or 3.

3. Vary the mantra. Try chanting the mantra OM or *AUM*. This sound is elongated as *ah-oh-ummm*. Each part of the sound is elongated. Repeat this seven times at the start of meditation. Then begin one of the focusing exercises from class 1, 2, or 3.

4. Did you know you can practice visual meditation with your eyes open? With your eyes slightly open, focus on the center of a flower or a candle flame while trying to have no other thoughts in your mind. After several minutes, close your eyes and begin your focusing exercise from class one, two, or three.

   Try all these tips. And here's one more.

5. Smile during your meditation practice. Keep your eyes closed and smile. That lightens everything up and creates an inner brightness. ☺

16

MARRIED/PARTNERED, SINGLE LADIES

I've been single for a while and I have to say, it's going very well. Like…it's working out. I think I'm the one.

—Emily Heller

A few words on the married/partnered and single life.

Marriage and Partners

You may be married or in a partnership that is working well. Or perhaps the opportunity for a partner may present itself.

These are the teachings I've encountered.

Marriage can serve as a mutual shield. The partners can protect one another. In a male/female partnership, since the more dense, compact male subtle physical body is not as damaged when anger or negative thoughts and emotions are directed toward it, a man can serve as a shield for his female partner's more powerful but more sensitive subtle physical body, which is far more easily damaged by negative thoughts and emotions. The man does not have to be physically present. The shield is a psychic bond that builds up over time.

A woman shields her male partner from psychic manipulations he may not be aware of. She brings a powerful spark to the relationship that shields him. Her fluidity helps him to perceive existence in different positive ways. If there are children, the parents create a shield of power, love and humility and a nurturing environment in which children can grow.

How do relationships grow rather than disassemble over time?

The secret to enduring partnerships is giving. It sounds simple, but it is a root cause. Both partners need to be equally giving. As long as both partners are giving, the marriage or partnership endures. If one stops, the partnership fails.

What is meant by giving? Giving can take many, many forms. It doesn't mean giving yourself away or losing integrity. Rather, it's a state of mind.

Giving creates a happy mind state on the part of the giver. It can be physical—a gift of flowers. It can be a gift of kind and supportive words. It can be a compliment. It can be treating your partner to a dinner or movie or play you know they would love. It can involve a surprise gift to break through a deadlock or argument. It can mean being in a good mood, even when you don't want to be, to help your partner's state of mind.

You know you are giving correctly when you are energized by giving. If you get drained, it's not the right gift. Giving happens day in and out, and it works if both partners are engaged. Giving never gets tired or old because there is no end to positive, selfless giving and the pleasure that giving produces.

One of my married, meditating friends told me that she views her relationship with her husband as one of supporting each other's tasks, whether the tasks are family, health, jobs, or homemaking.

"If you take on a life partner," she said, "it counts for everything. It gets you through the daily hassles. For me, being married creates a sense of protection against the violence and negativity in the world. I married when I was well into my thirties. I used to pick horrible relationships, and then I learned. My husband is one thousand times nicer than me. There's no meanness in my husband. You have to look for someone with kindness in their soul. He is a giving person. The rest can be worked out."

Single Ladies—a Growing Demographic

You may be single, albeit seeking a partner, or you may have decided to go it alone and drop out of the hunt. It's OK to seek a partner as long as you don't trash yourself daily if you are alone. And it's 100 percent OK to be alone, as there are many ways to give back to the system.

Who invented the idea that alone is a problem? You work, you have friends, you have passions, and you have fun. Single is not a stigma, it's an honor. In the United States, over 50 percent of the population is single. It's not the single status that is the problem. It's the attitude.

Because even now, I hear and read the wailing:

> I don't want to be alone!
> I don't want to die alone!

I don't want to travel alone!

I don't want to make decisions alone!

This is mental conditioning, and it's not true.

If you have to shrink yourself into a small part of your being to date or engage with a partner, why do it? Why dress and act with a doll-like look and a less-powerful-than-the-guy manner? Why power yourself down? If you have to do that, why not just go to the same event, party, outing, or film on your own?

I recently attended the premiere of a snowboarding film in New York City. Wearing my marketing hat, I handed out free books to over fourteen-hundred young people who attended the event. The atmosphere was friendly and upbeat. My female meditating colleagues and I could tell which woman was in the early-dating phase versus who was single or married.

The early-stage dating ladies wouldn't take a book. They hung back and let their manly guy take the book. We had to lean over the table, look the fluffed-up gal in the eye, and say, "Here, you will like this book too." These were powerful, capable New York ladies acting like timid little girls so that a male date could perceive himself as a leader. Why?

Deep mental conditioning and fear of aloneness—these habits can turn career goddesses into relationship actresses. Lionesses should not feel compelled to act like kittens. This is time and power wasting.

I find "single" to be a beautiful life. I enjoy my career in the technology profession and appreciate my well-earned salary. I buffer my life with ownership/guardianship of several dogs, who bring unconditional love and constant humor into my life. I shield my being with nice places to live and beautiful places to visit. I spend time alone and pursue avid interests and involvement in projects and groups that do good work. I exercise. I love learning new things. I have fine friends who are married, partnered, or single.

Rose, one of my meditation students, went through a rough divorce and was terrified at the thought of singleness. She decided to give herself a six-month break before seeking a new partner. During that time, she joined a gym, enrolled in classes, took a new assignment at work, traveled on her own to Europe. After six months, she decided to stay away from online dating services for another six months, then another... She's still single, and I see her eyes sparkling.

Ultimately, for women, whether you are married, in a partnership, or single does not matter at all. What is important is to be mindful that your innate power level continues to grow no matter what your companionship status is.

17

HOW TO INCREASE YOUR POWER

> Step out of the history that is holding you
> back. Step into the new story you are willing
> to create.
>
> **—Oprah Winfrey**

Assuming truthfully that a woman's power level is equivalent to a tsunami, fully risen, capable of taking any form, how do you manifest that in your life?

As a fluid and inherently influential being, how do you raise your power level? Raising your power level does not consist of lots of abstract, lofty principles. The suggestions that follow are grounded and practical. You can use these suggestions throughout the day.

1. Make Lists

Take a piece of paper and draw a line down the center. On the left side, make lists of people, places, and events that have increased your energy (and thus your power level). This might include a vacation, a new pair of shoes, a promotion at your job, going to the gym, spending time with a friend.

On the right side, make a list of people, places, and events that have decreased your energy (and thus your power level). The list may include shopping at certain grocery stores, attending particular meetings, spending time with a particular person. If something on your list only happens once, you may not have found a drainage spot, but if variations of the list item happen repeatedly, then you have pinpointed a source of power loss.

By writing these power gains and losses down, you are building your ability to gain power and not lose it. You need to first understand where you are losing power in order to plug up the holes.

This is your private list. It will change, sometimes on a daily basis.

2. Observe

The notion that a woman has a much more fluid subtle physical body and a man has a more condensed subtle physical body is observable. I see it 24/7 with every girl and boy, man, and woman I meet. It's obvious to me. Some of my favorite observation spots are places where people are relaxed—parks, coffee shops, hotel lobbies, grocery stores, and restaurants. You should simply start to observe.

Observe women. This is easier to do in younger women, before the subtle physical body has started to wear down, usually due to far too many openings to negative energy. See if you can sense instances when a woman's movement, the way she processes information, the way her emotions affect her, her spontaneity, the way she deals with people are consistent with a more lithe and fluid inner life force. The young women you observe probably have no idea how powerful they can be, but the power is there, like a wave that can become a tsunami.

Then look at men and see that they are vibrating differently. They are more fixed and contained. Their energy radiance seems more grid-like and subdued. Two men speaking together make this easier to notice. Pieces of the shining grid interlock.

In every case, I see that the women possess an inner current that is unlike their male counterparts. This is a no-blame situation, and no superiority is implied. However, the observation will show a clear gender difference.

All observation can be done quietly, using your intuition as well as your eyes

3. Spend Time Alone in Nature

You can sit alone in nature in a park where other people are. Or you may find a beautiful open space. Find a nice spot and sit down and relax a little bit. Take some slow, deep breaths. Just sit there and enjoy the rippling of the water (if you're near a lake or the ocean or the sea) or the stillness of the earth or the sound of the wind.

Look around and feel the abundant beauty. Even if you have a busy life and a family, you should ideally find time to be alone in nature, even for thirty minutes, at least once a week if not more often. You need to do this to build up your power level, to get in touch with who you are. Please be streetwise. Do not do anything unsafe.

If you're always surrounded by other people, you're always being imprinted by their thoughts and feelings, and you're not allowing a time for renewal and clearing. If there's no beautiful natural setting near you, spending time alone wherever you may be, even in a living room or bedroom, will help a bit. I think finding a spot to be alone on the upper floors of a high-rise building works-- you are away from the thoughts and feelings of others. Spending quiet time alone is a power enabler; you process your transformations and allow more balance and insight into your life.

4. Practice a Martial Art

Martial arts are not just for other people, young people, or kids. They are ideal for you. Going to a martial arts studio is important and delightful. All women and girls should learn at least one form of the martial arts. There are many styles, and they are usually taught by committed instructors.

The martial arts require you to use your mind and body together in a synchronized way that's conducive to building up your power level. And they also give you something very practical and special. If you ever do get caught in a compromising situation, you would have tools to deal with it. You would not feel helpless.

When I lived in New York, I studied tae kwon do with a very accomplished woman. Master Mineo, a sixth-degree black belt, told me that one of her students, a petite woman in her early fifties, was riding in an elevator with two of her female business colleagues. They were all dressed for work in high heels and suits with straight skirts. A tall, burly man got on the elevator, and as soon as the door closed, he pulled out a knife and raised it over his head, gripping the knife with both hands as he menaced the three women. Master Mineo's student responded instinctively. She delivered a powerful front snap kick to the groin. The man fainted in pain. The three women walked off the elevator.

For women, a mental attitude of preparedness, which you would achieve with six months or less of martial arts training, is very empowering. Your awareness of a few good martial arts moves dissolves the feeling that you must have a man always with you because you feel physically weak or fearful. This is not about getting into street fights. With a few months of training, you can kick and run. You can do something to defend yourself and get the heck out of there. That's important for self-esteem.

There are many types of martial arts. From a power-building perspective, the style does not matter as much as the teacher.

You want nice, humble, skilled teachers and a friendly, happy feeling in an impeccably clean studio. After the first few classes, you'll find you'll be thrilled with your decision to learn. If you have been reading this book and are still unsure how to build up your innate power level, enroll in a martial arts class.

5. Break Routines

When we're kids, everything seems new. The world is exciting and fresh. But then when we get older, we build up routines. We drive the same way to work, we live in the same place, and we wear our hair the same way. We go to the same restaurants, hang out with the same people. We view or practice the same sports for years.

To break your routines and do something you have not done before is energizing and empowering. To build up your power level, make a conscious effort to switch things around.

Plan a vacation or day trips to new places, places that you can feel with your intuition and body, that have a lively and clearing quality. Change hairstyles, buy clothes you would not have purchased before. Try different classes and sports. Go to movies you normally would not see.

You are removing the mental confines that hold you in place and consciously bringing fresh input into your synapses. Do this constantly in fresh ways, and your power level will increase.

6. Break off Relationships that Drain You

If you are in a relationship that is very draining, you have to look at that and see if it can be changed or if it is something you wish to continue. If your power level is increasing, you will be getting new ideas for how to change draining relationships.

If you can't act on this suggestion at first, try others in this chapter. You'll find there are very direct results when you have more power in your life. Following many of the suggestions in this chapter will free you to get out of a draining relationship or at least find ways to make it considerably less draining.

Note that a draining relationship is one in which you are spending time with a partner who is jealous, competitive, violent, emotionally clogged, humorless, completely fixed in their own routines and not open to change.

Over time, people go through many transitions. The person you were drawn to may have shifted in different ways than you, or vice versa. The idea that one must have a partner to be happy is not true. Draining relationships can happen at work, in families, in casual but repetitive interactions.

If you can't just cut the cord, identify the situation and put up a mental shield. When circumstances permit, if the drain continues, you have to move on or away.

7. Continue your Education

Your mind needs education to be powerful. Education—challenging classes of any kind—is your ticket to much clearer, brighter states of mind.

If you can't make it to a physical class, you can take wonderful courses online. Classes exist in every area of knowledge, and the training ranges from five-minute videos to actual university enrollment.

If your career is not giving you the money and power you need, advancing your education is your ticket. Many areas of knowledge give online certifications. Certification and other programs help you train your mind to be sharper and continually excited about learning new things.

You can sign up for the easy stuff, but if you really want to raise your power level, increase the level of challenge in your education. Take a technical class—this is practical and fear-breaking.

Building your mind will help build your power level. People who become successful and respected in their professions dedicated the time and put in the effort to become highly educated and informed. Your educated mind is sharp and strong, ready to handle power.

> Education is the most powerful weapon which you can use to change the world.
>
> —Nelson Mandela

8. Build your Income Level

"You can never be too rich or too educated." That's what the young Buddhist teacher said. The rich part may surprise you because we think of wealth as somehow unspiritual. But his point was that in the twenty-first century, you need money to be powerful. Education and wealth are related.

These days, you need a platform to be heard. Your voice is powerful, and you want people to hear it. If you do not have volunteer assistance, you'll likely need to spend money to build up a team. Your motives may be to teach and help others, which is another reason to make money. Earnings can be used to support good causes.

The STEM (Science, Technology, Engineer–ing, Math) careers are perfect for women because they engage the mind and offer a lifetime of interesting, well-paying career opportunities. For the same time period, you can train to be a nurse (a low-paying profession that exposes you to a slew of depressed and angry people) or you can train to be a computer scientist and enjoy a fascinating, fast-paced profession for the rest of your life.

Computer boot camps offer programs that are only six months long, and they help you find your first job after you complete the study.

In technology, you can negotiate a salary that is as high as your male counterparts for the same work. Many companies in the STEM field are looking for qualified women.

One of my women friends is a computer coder. She loves coding. She says that when she writes computer code, she enters into beautiful planes of light and awareness she cannot even describe. Because she is so good at what she does, she earns $249 per hour as a consultant. My friend teaches coding for free to other women who want to get started in the field.

Her first job did not pay that well, but from her first job forward, she rose quickly to success and expertise in her field.

If you are in a low-paying, low-power profession (usually the ones that traditionally were considered "safe" for women), you can start to strategize on how to move out of it. Take one step at a time. Even learning how to type and word process may be the start of a new career path in computer science. Wherever you are in your career, don't settle.

Women are powerful technical people, designers, managers, artists, communicators, strategists, and businesswomen. We use our success to support other women in the workplace.

The workplace is often difficult to navigate in consistently positive ways. My Buddhist teacher once said that anything you dislike in another person is a quality you have within yourself. If, for example, you are upset about the promotion of another person in your company, while you did not get one, take a look inside yourself. If you had received the promotion, would you want others to be happy for you and respect your progress? And if you truly deserved that promotion, are you confident enough to go and ask for it anyway?

Where you work and earn money will always be a huge learning ground.

Mindfulness means you find the part inside yourself that is not jealous or competitive and you stop the envious thoughts at their inception, before they take hold.

To help others and wish well for others is a happy state of mind. To assist the progress of another woman in your business environment is the right thing to do. Her success bodes well for your own.

Goal:

JOIN THE WOMEN MILLIONAIRE'S CLUB!

Why not? In fact, these days it's the billionaire's circle you want to step into. You have the power.

9. Hassle the Details

Keeping the bills paid, the house clean, the drawers organized, the closets free of unnecessary clutter, the car in good shape—staying on top of life's details is an energy gain. It's important and it works. When you need an energy boost, straighten up the clutter in new ways. This is the theme of Marie Kondo's KonMari method, and it works.

When my cousin, a real estate agent, gets a new listing for a house, the first thing she and her associates do is "stage" the house. They get rid of all clutter and leave open, clean spaces that allow potential buyers to picture themselves in the house.

When you declutter your own spaces, you leave a space for your mind to travel to new places. It all works together. Organize, toss, clean. Buy new containers for your jumbled goods so they can become unjumbled. Doing this external cleaning changes your inner being. Fold the undies neatly so that every time you open the drawer, you get a visual perk.

The organized home and office are an energy builder; the overrun, cluttered environment is a drain.

10. Dress To Impress

This power-builder is about attracting the right kind of attention. You are dressing to blend with successful people. We are judged by our appearance. With our sensitive, fluid, subtle physical bodies, women easily pick up on the thoughts and feelings of others.

People judge you by your gender, skin color, age. These are the first impressions. Then come posture, hair, and clothing. Your goal in dressing well is not to draw unwanted attention (flashy or way-naked clothing) but to draw wanted attention – i.e., not much attention at all, but whatever comes your way is positive and approving. "S/he looks capable and professional." "S/he looks neat and pleasant."

Dress helps you bypass gender, age, and race and draws attention to what people really care about – appearance! To build your power, master the art of appearance. You don't have to dress like a fashion model, but you should become aware of what successful people in your field wear. If you can't afford designer versions, buy the good knockoffs. Dress to mitigate negative energy (typically sexual energy directed at women by men) and to enhance strength and skillfulness.

For women, this means clothing, hair, makeup, accessories, a way to walk and carry yourself that look professional, as if you were going to work in New York City. Chic but not gaudy.

This is part of breaking routines. Go to your local department store or hairdresser and ask for their help. State your goal and budget, and they will help you have fun with this power-raiser.

11. Be Fearless and Perseverant

In the people stories in this book, a combination of courage and perseverance is a common thread.

If you are lucky, a time comes in your life when a doorway opens and you can step through it, or not. Fear is what usually holds us back. When I look at my life, I see the times I let my mind talk me into not walking through a doorway, and I regret those times. Whatever mental reasons I came up with for not taking an opportunity that was offered to me, the real reason was fear, also a bit of laziness.

Here is good advice for yourself: don't listen to all your mental reasons not to do something. Listen instead to your gut, a deeper intuition, and make choices that will empower you and lead you to your goals. Such decisions and brave moves bring more power into your life. If you can't make up your mind right away, wait. You will reach the right decision when the time is right.

We read more and more stories about women leaders today. All of them had to overcome many types of fear: fear of being unworthy, fear of failure, fear of what their peers might think. Fear of doing things we believe in is part of that old, embedded programming women must overcome. For so long, women were taught to fear crossing any kind of boundary. Now we can inspire each other to leap over restrictive lines and create new maps for our journeys.

Fearless women are featured on magazine covers, and in articles, blogs, photos, films. No one, however, was born fearless. These women became fearless like Malala, like Simone Biles.

They persevered, and over time and with terrific effort, they became "overnight successes." My point is they had the inner energy to do so, the huge tsunami wave inside them. They tapped into it, rode it, and still do.

12. Laugh More

Don't forget to laugh. The Age of Women is dawning. "Rule the World (Girls)." Beyoncé said so.

There are few role models out there. We all need to cultivate balance, and humor lightens the load.

Female comedians like Iliza Shlesinger or Amy Wong make us laugh through female eyes. I like innocent humor for belly laughs: *Shrek*, *Up*, *Kung Fu Panda*. If you think you're too old to watch or revisit a great kids' film, please add that to your power-building list. In Zen this is called "beginner's mind." This means you approach everything with an alert, fresh attitude all the time.

Other fun and happiness power builders: Dance. New sports. Beach runs. Facials. Manicures and pedicures. It's true. Do you feel better afterward? Take the momentum and keep going.

We are combatting millennia of sexism and ignorance, but that doesn't mean we can't smile.

Practice Meditation and Mindfulness

Mindfulness is not a luxury. It is a necessity. This is the roadway to balance, intuition, and internal power. Download Zazen music and start to meditate. It's free, requires no special equipment but your mind, and after several days of regular practice, it works.

Feel free to try other ways of meditating. Whether Zen, Tibetan, Chinese, or American, there are so many flavors. If you can stop thought during meditation for longer and longer periods of time, you have found a good method.

By practicing mindfulness during the day, you extend the benefit of your meditation practice. You become aware of and delete those negative, doubting, draining thoughts from your mind. Similarly, delete negative, doubting, and draining people from your life. You know who they are.

13. Set Goals

Know that not everything happens at once, but if you have goals and persist, you will reach your goals. At which point it is time for new goals. Our being is fluid, and the nature of power is rapid change. With some advance strategy and strong focus, you will succeed at achieving your goals.

The items in this to-do list overlap, and many can be done at once. All of them release power in your being.

18

MEDITATION CLASS #5 — YOUR MEDITATION ENVIRONMENT

Once you get into the habit of meditating, you'll find it continually rewarding and empowering. Meditation is the ground zero of female empowerment.

Some reminders:

Sit to meditate for at least fifteen minutes before you start your day. An easy way is to set your alarm clock fifteen minutes earlier. Sit up straight, close your eyes, and begin your meditation practice.

It's nice to have a special spot where you meditate. Set up a nice table with fresh flowers, a candle, perhaps some objects that remind you of beautiful places and moments. Sit in front of that table so that you have something beautiful and inspiring to look at before and after meditation.

Sit up straight during meditation. To sit up straight, it's not necessary to sit cross-legged if that is not comfortable for you. You can sit on a chair, or you can sit on the floor with your legs straight out. The important point is that your back is straight and you are seated comfortably, wearing clean and comfortable clothes, and you've already had your shower or splashed cold water on your face if you just woke up.

I suggest you meditate to Zazen music whenever you can. It will take your mind to beautiful planes of awareness, and you'll feel the meditative consciousness of the highly advanced meditator who produced the Zazen music. Free downloads are available at www.ramameditationsociety.org/resources/type/music

Don't eat right before meditation because you'll get sleepy. When you end your meditation, don't hop up and rush back to your daily world. Take a few deeper breaths. After meditating, sit for a few more moments and feel gratitude. Try an inner bow to eternity. Those are beautiful ways to end your meditation.

Don't judge your meditation. Even if it seemed filled with thoughts, you still touched on some quiet moments. You will feel the benefits of meditation just by engaging in the practice.

These are some ideas. Why not start with the suggestions you resist the most?

19

BREAKUPS, BREAKTHROUGHS AND MINDFULNESS

> When you take risks you learn that there will be times when you succeed and there will be times when you fail and both are equally important.
>
> **—Ellen DeGeneres**

> Failure means you're finally IN the game.
>
> **—Abby Wambaugh**

Of course there will be flops and breakups. On the path to delightful power, there will be new discoveries, new realizations, new decisions. There will be shedding of old selves, old places, and people who are not supportive.

My friend Tammy started an inner-city rock music summer camp for girls eight years ago. The first year was a struggle for attendance, facilities, loans of instruments. She learned from every challenge, and the second year brought more paid attendance, different girl groups, a cool new structure. With each year, she improved the recognition and curriculum at the camp. Now, the waiting list grows, donated instruments abound, and returning students serve as mentors.

Every iteration of the camp revealed a time to shed old ideas that were not working and open doors to new people and opportunities.

There will be breakthroughs—moments where you "get it." You fully intuit and see what has held you down so far in your life, and you shake free of it. At other times, you feel held back—you may be holding yourself back. But perhaps it's not time to change yet.

You cannot plan a breakthrough. They come at odd times. Walking down a beach, watching a movie, observing coworkers and friends, under stress, reading, viewing or hearing about a trending news item—many situations can cause rapid change.

On the path to delightful power, if someone were to chart your mind state, it would be like a wave, up and down, with a rising median. When you meditate, the downs are not as deep and do not last as long. A proven result of meditation is the ability to change and adapt to new circumstances with minimum stress. You now have the tools to do this.

Breakups happen. Change happens. Growing into your vast, innate power level is about becoming the large wave, not being buried by it.

Practice mindfulness. Then you discover and undo all the ways that repressive old programming about women creeps into your life and your mind and the minds of other women. Try to identify it and toss it out. You may not be able to change others, but you can change yourself.

I like this mindfulness technique and use it a lot.

Whenever I feel stressed or anxious, or just way too caught up in thoughts, I simply take a deep breath. I focus on the in breath through my nose as it starts from my navel area then rises to my chest, up to the center of my forehead and up to several inches above my head. Then I exhale through my mouth, feeling the breath return down through the center of my forehead and my chest and the navel area. The whole time I am doing this, I try to have no thought in the mind other than a strong focus on my breath.

After three of four breaths, I find I am thought-free and am no longer in the grip of whatever thought/emotion/anxiety storm had engulfed me. I can truly breathe easily.

This mindfulness technique can be done at work, in your car, anywhere. Your eyes can remain open, and I usually do this practice with eyes open. It centers me every time.

Mindfulness with meditation is the sandblasting of seaweed off the bottom of the boat.

Continuing to carry around that weighty old programming is pretty grim. Consider the forty-four-year-old project manager—beautiful, not married, desperate to find a husband and have children. She computer dates with focus on finding a rich man. Her goal is to find someone wealthy who will take care of her and the babies they haven't had yet. She disdains her current life in pursuit of this outdated goal.

Consider the single executive who has not taken a vacation in three years. Why? Because she doesn't want to travel by herself.

Consider the twenty-eight-year-old office assistant who went out of her way to obstruct her new female boss, while she deferred to all the male executives in the office.

Consider the posses of millennial women going out together to bars to find men.

There is a twitter hashtag #notbuyingit. Many women need to adopt this hashtag as they become mindful of the old programming and influences that cause them to undermine other women or stop short of realizing their true power.

If you are angry at your life because you do not have a partner, you most certainly are not reaching your true power level.

Breakups involve breaking away from limiting people and mind states.

Breakthroughs are the heightened energy and happiness you feel when you change and challenge yourself and let go of an old, repressive belief system.

Mindfulness and meditation are fuel to make the change and realizations happen more deeply and quickly. Be mindful. Become aware of your thoughts and feel if they are even really yours. Do not absorb the thoughts and feelings of others, however they come your way—at work; in media such as video games, news articles, social media, TV and film; from your family or friends.

Here's a hashtag-in-waiting—#fuhgeddabouddit.

Forget about it. Don't bow to the old repression, Instead, use mindfulness to become the incredibly powerful tsunami that you are.

20

PEOPLE: MICHELLE OBAMA, JACINDA ARDERN

> As women, we must stand up for each other.
>
> **—Michelle Obama**

> I really rebel against this idea that politics has to be a place full of ego and where you're constantly focused on scoring hits against one another. Yes, we need a robust democracy, but you can be strong, and you can be kind.
>
> **—Jacinda Ardern**

Michelle Obama is exceptional, and she is grounded. She is powerful, and she seeks to share how she developed her power. In a talk to high school students in Washington, DC, Michelle shared that when she was in high school, some of her teachers told her she was setting her sights too high. They told her she was never going to get into Princeton.

"It was clear to me," Michelle wrote in her 2018 biography, *Becoming*, "that no one was going to take my hand and lead me to where I wanted to go. Instead, it was going to be up to me to reach my goal. I had to chart my own course."

She knew she needed the strongest academic record possible, and she explained she worked day and night to receive the best grades she could in all her classes.

"I knew," she said in a 2013 address to Bell Multicultural High School, "I had to present a very solid and thoughtful college application, so I worked late and got up early to work on my essays and my personal statement. I knew my parents would not be able to pay for my tuition so I made time to learn how to apply for financial aid and understand all the deadlines.

"Most importantly, when I encountered doubters, when people told me I wasn't going to cut it, I didn't let that stop me. In fact, it did the opposite. I used that negativity to fuel me, to keep me going. And at the end, I got into Princeton, and that was one of the proudest days of my life."

Michelle graduated magna cum laude with a sociology degree from Princeton. She went on to Harvard Law School and spent her early legal career working at the law firm Sidley Austin, where she met her future husband.

"Education is the key to freedom."

"Be bold with your intelligence."

"Be willing to take risks and learn from failure."

These statements are what Michelle tells young students. They apply to everyone. Michelle credits her education with every opening she has walked through thus far in her life. In her public career as First Lady, she became an icon of leadership. She demonstrated having fun, being unpretentious, remaining practical and balanced.

Now past the First Lady years, she says she will keep going and work on issues she cares about. She has the inner confidence and experience to do this. She is a strong, articulate role model for women. Her career timeline demonstrates how to raise and maintain an inner power level--new challenges, new creativity, working hard, and always raising the bar.

Women today are surrounded by doubters and female imagery that is significantly less than powerful. Women still struggle with self-doubt. Michelle's realization—doubters fuel her determination to succeed—is right on topic.

* * *

When I lived in New Zealand for a year and a half, Jacinda Ardern became the top candidate in the Labour Party for the role of prime minister. There are several major parties in New Zealand, and she seemed to emerge out of the blue to become head of one of them. But in fact, she had been working in political spheres since age eighteen. Her mentor was Helen Clark, the other woman Labour prime minister of New Zealand.

While spending time overseas, she worked for two years in the offices of Tony Blair. Upon her return, she became a member of Parliament and was appointed to prominent positions in the government. She was new to government, but when she became the Labour party leader, "Jacindamania" took hold. All the people in my little town of Paekakariki planned to vote for her. She began taking part in debates to present and defend her policies, and she wiped the floor with her male opponents, not only with sharp, take-no-prisoners debating style but also extremely sensible and articulate policies. She was fierce, and she won every debate. She also won the election. Her slogan was "Let's do this."

Now she had to deal with governing. She describes her main governing trait as "relentless positivity." Her areas of focus were (and are) homelessness, clean rivers, economic wellness, and the rights for indigenous people (the Maori). She and her team were proceeding to tackle these issues when, on March 15, 2019, New Zealand experienced a brutal attack on its Muslim population. An Australian-born white supremacist entered two Christchurch mosques and killed fifty people using an automatic rifle, an act of terrorism never seen before in that country. Ardern's response revealed power as it is meant to be used.

She went to Christchurch, a scarf covering her head, and warmly hugged all the mourners gathered in grief at the mosques.

In an interview for *The Guardian*, just weeks after the terror attack, she said, "Very little of what I did was deliberate. It's intuitive. I think it's just the nature of an event like this. There is very little time to sit and think. You just do what feels right… I just thought about sentiments, and what I thought needed to be conveyed."

Four days later, speaking to parliament, she pointedly refused to speak the name of the man who did it. ("He is a criminal. He is an extremist, but he will, when I speak, be nameless.") Gun law reforms, intended to ban all semiautomatic firearms, were expedited with cross-party support.

Two weeks later at a memorial service for the victims, Ardern received a standing ovation. "We each hold the power, in our words and in our actions, in our daily acts of kindness," she said. "We are not immune to the viruses of hate, of fear, of other. We never have been. But we can be the nation that discovers the cure."

Ardern told *The Guardian*, "People have remarked upon the way we've responded [to the terror attack], but to me there was no question. You need to remove some of the politics sometimes and just think about humanity. That's all."

How do women rule a nation? Fluidly. With wisdom, common sense, intuition, strength, bravery. All the qualities you would expect of a person who is fueled by a tsunami, fully risen.

21

VISUALIZATION TECHNIQUE

Sit comfortably in your meditation spot or where you will not be disturbed. Close your eyes. Imagine that directly in front of you is a huge wall of water, one hundred feet high, stretching out of your range of vision in either direction. The wave has not plunged down yet, nor will it. It remains risen, quivering with power, able to crash down and take any form and plunge forward, but not at this stage. Its power is fully exposed in an awesome display of might. It has deep lucent colors of light green, turquoise, and iceberg blue, and all its colors are laced with light, glimmering and shining with beauty.

Gaze into the center of the wave. Feel the power of the wave. Feel that it is your own inner power.

Feel yourself using this power to help others.

Feel yourself using this power to learn more and bring more to your work or study.

Feel yourself using this power to meditate.

Make friends with the tsunami wave, risen. Its astounding power is yours. Feel that it is your treasure and gift to magnify the power of this wave with the power of the tsunami energy of other women.

Do this for several minutes, then slowly open your eyes.

22

VIKING LEADERS

Of course there have been powerful women warriors. Recent history has erased or ghosted most of them. That's why I liked it when archaeologists tested the DNA of the skeleton of an eleven-hundred-year-old Viking warrior.

"Viking" is a catchall term for the people who came from Scandinavia—what is now Norway, Denmark, and Sweden—between the eighth and eleventh centuries. They are also known as the Norse or Norsemen [or Norsewomen]. They had a notorious reputation as raiders and pirates of the medieval age; their raids were fierce and long running.

The Viking skeleton was found preserved in an underground cave in Birka, Sweden. The warrior had been buried with full fighting clothes and weaponry, two horses, and gaming apparatus for testing war strategies. This demonstrated leadership of Viking troops. Historians assumed the skeleton was male.

Recently, DNA tests revealed that the warrior-Viking leader was a woman. As a friend of mine pointed out, "They were probably all women."

As soon as the findings of the female Birka warrior were released, controversy ensued. The main argument was that a warrior couldn't be a woman. The female researcher who led the DNA testing, however, continued to assert that the warrior was a woman. The skeleton was without question female.

"I must say I thought that we had come much further than that; I was surprised by the reactions we had to the article,"[6] said Charlotte Hedenstierna-Jonson, a professor of archaeology at Uppsala University in Sweden who coauthored the 2017 paper about the find.

Hedenstierna-Jonson predicted that as more Viking archaeologists begin to challenge their assumptions about gender in their work, they might look for more female Vikings who held special positions like the Birka female

---

[6] https://www.history.com/news/viking-warrior-female-gender-identity

warrior did, and perhaps even discover that some previously discovered graves were misidentified.[7]

Hedenstierna-Jonson and her colleagues also considered gender identity. "There are many other possibilities across a wide gender {identity] spectrum," she said, "some perhaps unknown to us, but familiar to the people of the time. We do not discount any of them."[8]

The seeming audacity of discovering a female Viking leader and disbelief concerning the findings show how far we still have to go in reclaiming history. As women and men continue to bust the overt, disempowering sexism that tainted the recording of history, we will start to enjoy a much wider range of role models.

---

[7] Ibid.

[8] https://www.history.com/news/viking-warrior-female-gender-identity

23

KNOWLEDGE

"Women bring a different way of thinking; a cooperative spirit; a gift for 'reading' people; patience; empathy; networking abilities; negotiating skills; a drive to nurture children, kin, business connections and the local and world community; an interest in ethnic diversity and education; a keen imagination; a win-win attitude; mental flexibility; an ability to embrace ambiguity; and the predisposition to examine complex social, environmental, and political issues with a broad, contextual, long-term view.

As the female mind becomes unleashed on our modern world, societies will benefit—even in lands where it is currently shackled."

—Helen E. Fisher, Ph.D.

As the young Buddhist educator said many years ago, when you are trying to suppress a people, you must convince them of their own powerlessness.

That is exactly what happened to women. When you rise from powerlessness, relatively small victories seem great. But are they?

I like to keep an eye on the news. There's a spotlight now on women's power and prowess in history, politics, sports, business, and many other arenas. Women buried by history are moving into center stage. The many aspects of female power are joining together in diverse ways. You can use your readings and viewings to help you see how far women have come and where they still need to go.

To revive your own sense of female power, it helps to know you cannot be fooled into accepting powerlessness, that it was a sham all along.

Have you seen the Netflix TV series *The Ascent of Woman*? It is a well-researched documentary on the repression of women since 7500 BC, highlighting the short-lived instances when women broke out of the binding box. There are not that many occurrences, which is why it is so critical for women to understand what has happened and then unite worldwide.

I like a classic book titled *When God Was a Woman* by Merlin Stone. Published in 1978, Stone's writing sparked much of the feminist movement. I found it fascinating that women-led cultures had literally been buried or misrepresented in male-dominated societies. The message is still accurate today.

Knowledge is good; more knowledge is even better.

Tsunamis are caused by massive natural events such as earthquakes, volcanoes, an asteroid strike. Every time we see and read reports of women gaining in influence and power, making breakthroughs in their various careers, having a broad social impact, achieving unprecedented victories in sports, pioneering in science and technology, I feel and view it as adding to the wave.

The Earth is racing toward climate self-destruction. What can we do? It is critical for women to work together to build their vast power levels, to provide their healing force to the planet. We can lead and act with intuition, a faster and more accurate way to react.

Women can use insights provided by their powerful energy bodies to feel untruth and heal.

Both men and women have everything to gain by understanding their relationship to power. Men have been stripped of their loving nature, with their kindness and humility largely repressed. Women have had their power held down, laughed at, and distorted.

Times are changing, as they must to heal the planet.

The ultimate power of women is enlightenment, a spiritual and metaphysical state of being that does not preclude the world but is all encompassing. Early in these pages, I wrote of a profound Buddhist teaching—women can meditate and move the kundalini energy (life force) more readily through their body than men because women have a fluid, supple energy body that is conducive to higher meditation. Why, then, have more women not attained enlightenment?

The answer is—repression in the form of inappropriate marriage, social pressure, mental programming, violence, lack of access to education, and old habits. We are now in a time of transition. Change is occurring on all fronts for women, but the violence and anger toward women remain.

Women today can take stock, create an inner inventory of their fears, and understand the roots of their historic lack of self-worth and confidence. They can look to other powerful women and learn.

Just know that after (and during) the work it takes to become the most powerful, self-confident, economically self-sufficient, and beautiful woman you can be, you can do one more thing. You can sit to meditate. You can close your eyes, use a focusing technique to stop (initially slow) your thoughts, and begin to experience fields of light, planes of awareness that are beyond delightful, that will bring a smile to your face as you meditate. It doesn't take that long. You can go there now.

I support and am inspired by the active, worldwide community of women working to assert and reclaim their power. I look forward to hearing more about an active, global community of men asserting their love and humility.

Women around the world are uniting to throw off every form of repression.

Women, you are far, far more powerful than you realize.

**YOU ARE
THE TSUNAMI,
FULLY RISEN.
DO NOT FORGET.**

LIZ LEWINSON

Liz Lewinson is an award-winning author, speaker, teacher, technologist, strategic planner, and feminist.

She is Vice President and Treasurer of The Frederick P. Lenz Foundation for American Buddhism. She leads the grant category titled "Women in Buddhism."

Liz has authored three books--*American Buddhist Rebel: The Story of Rama - Dr. Frederick Lenz; Women, Meditation, and Power*, and *The Power of the Loving Man* – with additional book and audiobook projects underway.

She began her career as a freelance journalist and soon segued to Hollywood public relations, landing A-list clients in a number of entertainment sectors. Within an eight-year period, she became Senior Vice President of Marketing and Public Relations for Tri-Star Television and Stephen J. Cannell Productions. At Cannell, she managed television series, film, talk shows, and TV specials.

Intrigued by the field of computer science, she left public relations in the early 90s and took in-depth training in computer science. She was soon managing complex, multi-million dollar I.T. projects for top Wall Street firms.

In early 2016, she accepted a job in New Zealand as Communications Manager at Utilities Disputes, an ombudsman office for consumers wishing to resolve disputes about electricity, gas, water, and more. In late 2017, she returned to the U.S. to take on more responsibilities at the Lenz Foundation.

Through her company, Skye Pearl, she currently focuses on creating powerful and meaningful global communications through books, audiobooks, film, and other media. To learn more about Liz and her work, visit www.lizlewinson.com.

 www.facebook.com/LizLewinsonAuthor

 www.instagram.com/LizLewinson

 www.twitter.com/LizLewinson

www.ingramcontent.com/pod-product-compliance
Lightning Source LLC
Chambersburg PA
CBHW070426010526
44118CB00014B/1922